THE

GOLDEN BUDDHA

CHANGING

MASKS

AN OPENING TO TRANSFORMATIVE THEATRE

THE

GOLDEN BUDDHA

CHANGING
MASKS

AN OPENING TO TRANSFORMATIVE THEATRE

MARK OLSEN

GATEWAYS / IDHHB, INC. PUBLISHING

Published by:
Gateways Books and Tapes / IDHHB, Inc.
P. O. Box 370
Nevada City, California 95959
www.gatewaysbooksandtapes.com
530-477-8101; 800-869-0658
FAX: 530-272-0184

Cover Design: iTRANSmedia

Previous ISBN 0-89556-083-6 ISBN 0-89556-058-5 (pbk.)
ISBN-13: 978-0-89556-083-4 ISBN-10: 0-89556-083-6

Library of Congress Cataloging-in-Publication Data

Olsen, Mark, 1954-
Golden Buddha changing masks : an opening to transformative theatre / by Mark Olsen. -- 2nd ed. rev.
p. cm.
Includes bibliographical references and index.
ISBN-13: 978-0-89556-083-4
ISBN-10: 0-89556-083-6
1. Acting--Psychological aspects. 2. Acting--Religious aspects. I. Title.
PN2071.P78O47 2006
792.02'8019--dc22
2006031310

*This book is dedicated to Carla and Ben
and to all my teachers and students
who have provoked, guided, and inspired me
to keep searching.*

Dear Reader of the Revised *Golden Buddha Changing Masks*:

We at Gateways Books are sure that you are going to enjoy this book and that you will find it both edifying and enlightening—whether you are an actor, director, theater-goer, or simply an interested reader. We would before you even begin your read like to apologize for a set of editorial and typographic errors in the book which are NOT the responsibility of the author, Mark Olsen, but rather our professional responsibility at Gateways Books.

You will find on page 105 a series of misspelled words and on pages following some other problems in typography and spacing of the text. Note particularly that on page 169, in the first line of the exercise <u>Playing an Action,</u> that the sentence should read as follows:

Effectively defining and playing an action is the basis for all good acting.

We hope you will overlook these minor flaws and concentrate on Mark Olsen's rich and nuanced updating of most of the chapters in this book, especially his new "Author's Introduction" and the revised "Practical Exercises." Be assured that we will correct all these errors in the next printing of this book, and we will welcome any feedback from you, the readers, on what you particularly like and don't like about this edition, especially in the classroom and actor-training context.

Thanks for your interest and your compassion,

Iven Lourie, Editor
Gateways Books

TABLE OF CONTENTS

PREFACE

In *The Golden Buddha Changing Masks*, Mark Olsen asks, "Why should inspiration and growth in the spiritual dimension be relegated only to poets, musicians, painters, and dancers? The actor, too, has the right and the means to enter through the mysterious gates and struggle to awaken."

In this ground-breaking and stimulating book, the author reminds us of the spiritual longings that gave rise to the craft of acting in the distant past; he skillfully details how the spiritual path to awakening parallels, in important aspects, the path of the actor as he prepares his body, voice, intellect, and spirit for the practice of his craft. In an astonishing new look at Stanislavski, Olsen uncovers the strong influence of the perennial wisdom traditions, including the Hindu, on the man who formulated the most influential acting theories of the modern Western theater.

Above all, in an era in which mass entertainment and commercial necessity seem at times to have all but obliterated the spiritual practice and ritual that brought the theater to life, Mark Olsen reminds actors and people of the theater of who we really are, and what we may yet become, if we have sufficient discipline and courage.

This book is sure to be greeted with joy and relief that, at last, we have been reminded of the "road less travelled" that was there all along, waiting to be reclaimed by a new generation of artists.

For those eager to start the journey, the book is full of practical exercises and suggestions for beginning, one step at a time, to reconnect their artistic energies to the ancient sources of power and joy.

Ruby Allen, Ph.D.
Jungian Analyst and former Director of Voice and Speech Training
The Florida State University
Asolo Conservatory of Professional Actor Training

E.J. Gold, *The Troubadour,* Pen & Ink,
pencil signed, 11" x 15", Rives BFK,
© 1987 Heidelberg Editions International.

INTRODUCTION

The first edition of this book began with the statement: "There are no accidents." It was meant to provoke questions about the cosmic nature of our experience and to get readers wondering about the patterns and random acts in their own lives. The statement inclines the reader toward an inner inventory and a measurement of experiences and memories compelled by the phrase. It's a common device and one of many used by those maverick teachers and colleagues who have helped shape my own unusual brand of teaching through the years.

Occasionally this phrase and others like it will produce the desired effect. People perplexed by the statement and other similar pronouncements in the book ask me about them, hoping to tack down my exact meaning. Something rumbled within them and they were intent upon resolving that rumbling. I have always relished those moments when a person pieces together various thoughts and emotions into a question. Most often the answer is embedded within the form and content of the question itself, making the answer of the exchange relatively easy. The agitation of a good question derived from an encounter with this book is music to my ears and one of my central motives for writing it.

Questions are roving streams of thought that are attached to rivers of deeper thoughts, and they in turn can be linked to a whole tidal wave of very powerful inner intentions. And just as there are all kinds of thoughts, there are all kinds of questions. They can topple out of a topsy-turvy mind in a chaotic ramble or bubble up from deep within the innermost part of a person's necessity. Over the years I've come to appreciate the power of formulating a question. I much prefer to hear a good question than to hear any version of an answer. The questioning is a real effort, a workout for the inner journey, and it removes the person from the comforts of outer distractions to the irritations of the inner search. Because I know how important it is to formulate a question that would have consequences capable of attending to real necessity, I have linked this book to those traditions that refuse to settle for answers that simply sound like answers.

So, I began with: "There are no accidents." It is an odd statement, really, and certainly ironic coming from a man who has survived several very serious car accidents. So, what does that mean, "no accidents"? Is that just another way of saying, "It's all good"? Is it well meaning but exaggerated new age romanticism? The statement could easily make you roll your eyes because, obviously, there are accidents. We experience them, we see them happen all the time, and as a result we intuit a kind of accidentalness about the cosmos; as if chaos and random order are inexplicably woven into our lives. And yet, at the same time, the accidental events often come with an intimation of a larger unseen plan. Some accidents seem to have an uncanny timing and on occasion they come with uniquely satisfying by-products or results. This is indeed a paradox.

From my present level of experience, I find there are zones in which, through inattention or unconsciousness, one can come under the influence of what might be called the "law of accident." Hapless participants in that zone suddenly find themselves out of synch with the intended energy flow while events take on a jagged and unwieldy character. You snooze, you lose. And, of course, there are unpredictable and seemingly random acts of nature, of violence, of kindness, and of the Las Vegas slot machine jackpot. In the face of all that, how can I assert that there are no accidents?

In order to answer this question, I need to take a short scientific tangent. If you are not particularly science-minded, I ask you to bear with me through the next few paragraphs. I will attempt to walk you gently through some rather stunning insights drawn from recent developments in physics. If you enjoy scientific inquiry, you may already have had exposure to these discoveries. Either way, please hang in there so you can connect the dots of these ideas and come to appreciate what I find to be one of the more elegant attributes of our cosmos.

I'll begin by revealing that in 1982, a research team at the

University of Paris, led by French physicist Alain Aspect, discovered that under certain circumstances subatomic particles such as electrons are able to communicate instantaneously with each other regardless of the distance separating them. It doesn't matter whether they are 10 feet or 10 billion miles apart. Since this breaks with Einstein's notion that nothing can travel faster than the speed of light without breaking the time barrier, some explanation was in order. This has led some to consider a radical shift in how we view reality.

One of those views considers the possibility that our whole universe could, in fact, be a very sophisticated hologram. Briefly, a hologram is a three-dimensional photograph made with the help of a laser. The object to be photographed is bathed in laser light (near perfect coherent wavelengths) and the reflection laser light (the wavelengths now disturbed by the experience of striking an object) and both sources end up on a photographic plate. The finished plate is nothing special to see, but when a laser beam illuminates it, a three dimensional image of the object appears in space. What is even more remarkable is that every part of the photographic plate possesses the information about the object so that if shattered, any single piece can be illuminated and the object will appear. The whole is in every part.[1]

Scientists have come to witness that within each piece of creation there are smaller units that, although only parts of the larger piece, are also representations of the whole. The whole is itself a unit for an even bigger piece and so on and so forth, nested one within another like Chinese boxes. DNA is one obvious example of that principle. Noted author, Arthur Koestler, as well as the American philosopher and writer, Ken Wilber, refer to each unit of creation, each box you might say, as a "holon." Each whole unit is a part of another whole unit, so it is simultaneously a part and a whole.

In similar fashion, our experiences in this multi-layered universe are shaped by a variety of inexorable laws acting and reacting in a holonic and hologramic way within the multifaceted corridors of relative time/space events. Those laws flow with and nudge along the subatomic event panorama into manifestations that reflect and are guided by our deepest thoughts and desires. Events in the world are electromagnetic, quantum level processes that emerge into a certain magnification capable of our apprehension and then transmute, going up or down the scale; turtles all the way up and all the way down.

This is a very old idea found in many ancient traditions. In the Vedantic lineage, for example, as currently espoused by the venerable Maharishi Mahesh Yogi, there is the idea of a unified field of energy called pure consciousness. This pure consciousness is a supercharged energy state of complete and utter wavelessness: a quantum energy field of all possibilities, unmoving, featureless, and un-manifest. Deep thoughts, images, ideas, mantras of all kinds can and do evolve into refined energy charges capable of entering the field of *pure consciousness* with much of the thought or intent intact. Once there the un-manifest energy field, disturbed by the introduction of a thought, transforms the thought into manifest energy.

According to the precepts of this ancient wisdom, the events of our lives are being arranged as it were in a field of profound awareness living well below ordinary consciousness. Thus, the whole world is indeed within a grain of sand, but on some level that grain is a manifestation or an outgrowth into form from a formless idea, from a thought or intention within a certain spectrum of energy.

Now consider the notion that when in the flow of full attention, that is, attention using the entire apparatus of the being, events can take on uniquely-patterned synchronicity and unfold with uncanny elegance. Most of us have had peak moments of surprising lucidity or effectiveness. During the experience, it is as if nothing can go wrong. However, if your attention wavers creating a momentary "oops," you enter the harsh and often inelegant law of accident. At this point, the sensation of flowing within a timeless dimension of grace and charm suddenly evaporates and reality seems strangely choppy.

Once, while meditating in a chamber with advanced transcendental meditation acolytes, my awareness traveled to deeper and deeper levels of rest. My breathing and pulse slowed to an astonishing degree while my attention remained lively and vivid. This journey revealed increasingly subtle layers of impulse and thought until at one point, everything went completely empty. The engine sound of life simply stopped. It was as if someone simply pulled a switch and the whole organic hum of creation just switched from "on" to "off," and I entered a deep and utterly blissful all-pervading silence. The silence was so startling, so unlike any silence I had ever experienced in ordinary life that I quickly opened my eyes, fully expecting to discover that the electricity in the building had been shut off or New York City had just had a blackout, plunging all of us into deep darkness. To my surprise, the others were blissfully meditating in the soft illumination of the electric light. Nothing in the outer dimension had changed. "Oops," I thought, "I accidentally bumped myself out of Samadhi." This is not unlike an actor or musician or athlete who hits an extraordinary peak moment and then ruins it with a sudden comment on the moment. The minute an actor says to himself, "Wow, I'm really in the moment," it's all over. The flow is broken and the law of accident ensues.

Nevertheless, I sometimes ask: was this "accident," this fall from grace, intended? Was the event spectrum laced with speed bumps that serve as necessary shocks? Are these accidents part of a larger plan and if so can they truly be considered accidental? Is the choppy reality less important than the silent flowing harmonious one in the grand scheme of things? Is there, in fact, a grand scheme or is the universe being created like a magic flashlight shining in the dark, creating creation moment by moment as we live it?

There, much clearer now, isn't it? Aren't you glad I took the time to elucidate the idea behind the statement with which I began my first version of this book?

Most probably this book has come to your attention because you are in some way linked to the performing arts and have also been exposed to one or more of the lines of esoteric spiritual teachings that lead toward self-realization, enlightenment, or religious devotion. In short, you are a seeker.

My journey to the first edition and now this newly revised version was like a strange cross-country, cross-dimensional, skiing event. I made my way up and down this particular little mountain with one ski traveling in the world of the professional and educational theatre, the other traveling in the world of religious technology and philosophic endeavor. There were times while skiing the slopes of those experiences when I dropped a ski or I found myself in real danger of splitting apart, but by riding the center, picking myself up after the wipe outs, staying in the flow for as long as possible, I continued on course.

Perhaps it was the unpredictable travels of my childhood, or perhaps it was my own natural, but relentless urge to explore my inner landscape that shaped me as a young boy. Or, perhaps it was the influence of the Arizona desert and the compassion of the Native Americans I encountered there. Whatever it was, something planted me firmly in both the world of the spiritual quest and the world of theatre, driving me to seek teachings and teachers from all traditions. I came to know western Zen, Transcendental Vedanta, the Kabbalah, Taoism, Mahayana Buddhism, American Sufism, Evangelical Christianity, Esoteric Christianity, high and low-tech Shamanism. I have studied Stanislavski-based acting, both Meisner and Method, as well as Meyerhold, Brecht, Mask, Mime, Roy Hart Voicework, Michael Checkov's psychological gesture, Shakespeare, Greek, and Commedia Del 'Arte. I am a professional actor, director, and a nationally recognized movement specialist and fight director. I have been tenured at three major academic theatre departments, provided movement expertise for The Alley Theatre, Dallas Theatre Center, New York Shakespeare Festival, Hartford Stage Company, Pennsylvania Center Stage, Theatreworks, Houston Shakespeare Festival, and have taught at the Omega Center, the New York Open Center, Houston Grand Opera, the National Fight Director's Workshop and the Public Theatre in New York. All of this activity, all of this dedication and searching has made my life a wonderful adventure and has revealed to me the humor and terror and delicious synchronicity of our existence here.

Once, when one of my teachers was giving a workshop in New York, we took a break from the special movements we were learning, and as we sat, perusing some photos from the previous day's events, a young woman from the workshop entered the space. The teacher looked up at her and said, "What?" She looked back at him and remarked, " Coming here to this workshop, I feel like I'm being hypnotized." He smiled and said, "You are assuming you weren't hypnotized before coming here." That exchange struck me like a bolt of lightening. "That's it!" I thought. "That's the horror of man's time on earth. Unless we strip away the delusion filters and manage to sneak past our conditioning, we will continue to fall hypnotically into the world the way we fall into a book or a film."

Later that same workshop, and again, during a break, I was doing my Tai Chi form in a secluded section of the workspace. The teacher, with his bald pate and sly, knowing smile, walked past me, turned and said, "How will that help you in the Bardos?" I played it off as if it were a joke, as if he was implying somehow that Tai Chi had no long-range spiritual value. To my surprise, and now, today, to my profound gratitude, he followed up, turning the question into a real one, "No, I mean, how will Tai Chi help you in the Bardos?" The exchange was disarmingly simple, but in it rested the crux of a life's work.

One day, years before, while bounding down a flight of stairs in the theatre department where I worked as a teaching assistant, I came across a flyer announcing a summer mime workshop. I was already steeped in the techniques and beauty of mime and was forever sneaking into the theatre space after hours to delve into that fun and inspiring world. So, it took no time at all for me to decide to apply. This was no ordinary mime workshop, however, and the teacher was not just a keeper of technical movements. His approach was an outgrowth of his Kabbalistic lineage, a word and tradition I knew absolutely nothing about at the time.

I was hoping to get more skills in order to enhance my professional marketability. What I got, however, was far more valuable: an introduction to a way of working and a way of living that has become my life's joy.

Shortly after arriving and settling into my housing, I called the office and asked if I could visit the teacher. Mr. Avital was in and agreed to see me later that afternoon. I walked in the crisp mountain air to his apartment, placed my shoes in the rack just outside the doorway and entered into a unique inner sanctum. The teacher was seated at a desk, typing away and singing a song in Hebrew and smiling in a relaxed impish manner. I waited there for what seemed to be ages, until, having no other choice, I simply relaxed and surrendered to waiting. Soon afterwards, Mr. Avital finished his writing, turned in his chair and looked at me with complete attention. He seemed to be sizing me up, and, after several minutes of this, he smiled a huge grin and said, "So, Mr. Professor."

I was taken aback. What was this "professor" stuff? I was an actor and had no plans to be a professor, so his reference was not entirely welcome. Still, he persisted. "Mr. Professor. I see that you come from 2222 Orville Street – like the Wright brothers, yes? You want to fly away, Mr. Professor?"

I didn't know how to respond. I think I sat there and just laughed uncomfortably. He went on. "That is a lot of 2's. Twenty-two, twenty-two. Hmmmmmm. So, Mr. Professor, I notice here on your application that you are twenty-two years old, yes?"

"Yes."

"Good. That is good. Did you know that there are twenty-two days in this workshop?"

"No"

"That's right. Twenty-two days. And how many people do you think there are in this workshop?"

"A. . . twenty-two?"

"That's right. Twenty-two people. Did you happen to notice the number on my doorway as you came in?"

"Twenty-two."

"That is correct. Twenty-two. And now, Mr. Professor, how many letters are there in the Hebrew alphabet?" Taking a wild guess I said, "Twenty two?" "That's right! So you see, Mr. Professor, you are meant to be here!"

And indeed I was. The workshop was extraordinarily transformative. For the first time I began to realize that all of my many unusual experiences in childhood, the dreams, the callings, the encounters with unexplained phenomena, were all part of a wider area of research, one that harkens back into antiquity and yet remains very much alive today.

I had numerous memorable experiences that summer: the scent of roses in the air, learning to meditate, applying my imagination in profound ways, and having for the first time a sense of community that transcended the workaday world. It was delicious.

Late one night, after a day of work, a small group of us, perhaps four or five, entered into a silent and very attentive improvisational space. We shared pantomimic inventions and communed in silent behavior so simple and true we all became, for lack of a better phrase, kinetically telepathic. It was quite amazing. Consider that moment when you and a friend say the same thing or have the same thought at exactly the same time. Now, imagine that extending on and on, no one daring to comment for fear of breaking the spell.

At one point we were all moving an invisible ring in the space. It was about three inches in diameter, reflective chrome in color and cool to the touch. As you can tell, the ring became increasingly real to us as we moved it around the space in every possible configuration. Eventually, we all were inside the ring and moving it along at chest level from left to right. It will sound exaggerated, but truly, we were so absorbed in our experience that the ring actually appeared to us. It even transformed from a solid shape into a warm, well-defined beam of light encircling us. Our hands were grabbing it in perfect synchrony and moving it along, keeping it rotating gently around us. Then, without a sound and at the exact same time, we lifted the ring over our heads and stepped out of the circle, facing one another. The open astonishment on each of our faces was unforgettable. Gradually we diminished the ring until it was about the size of a serving platter and then, again without any words or special signs to one another, we all simultaneously tossed the ring up into the infinite beyond above our heads, through the roof and out into the cosmos.

This moment was so special, so intimate, so charged with magic that none of us spoke. We simply looked deep into each other's eyes, contained our euphoria, and walked to our respective domiciles.

Many years after that event, and after having had several similar experiences, I was teaching a theatre class at the New York Open Center. During a break, two of the participants came up to me and told me of an experience they had had recently. Apparently, the two of them have long been hacky-sack buddies. (For those of you not au courant, hacky-sack is a game where a small bean bag is kicked aloft and kept from hitting the ground by the action of kicking it with the feet or knees. In pairs or groups, it is kept aloft and passed from person to person with the intention being simply to keep it bouncing and keep it from landing on the floor or earth).

These two friends were on a cross-country drive and in Arizona they took a break from the drive in order to play hacky-sack before dark. Finding a remote spot with an excellent view of the impending sunset, they began to play as usual. They played and played, the hacky-sack never touching the ground. They continued to play and still they seemed to have just the right timing and just the right moves to prevent the sack from faltering or falling. The colors of the sky began to turn and before they knew it, they both were in a zone whereby their movements seemed to be in slow motion, they were both breathing deeply and sending this sack high into the air and across great distances and still, no break in the flow.

They played like this until the sun set and they could no longer see the hacky-sack. Never before or since have they experienced such a profound, seemingly flawless connection. It was as if their reality suddenly became fluid, alive, responsive, flowing, and magical.

Having had my own versions of that experience I was able to put it into some sort of perspective for them, so they would be free to leave it behind. Nevertheless, it was just one more validation that there is more going on than meets the consensus eye.

These events are not only reserved for pals or people in workshops. I used to perform mime in Los Angeles in the courtyard of the Dorothy Chandler Pavilion. One evening, as the public was arriving in their tuxedos and gowns, I was performing with a very pleasurable sense of ease and authority. My mime technique was excellent, my inner connection was full and my timing impeccable. The viewers lavished me with praise, applause, and also lots of cash. At one point, a young wide-eyed little boy drifted toward me. I opened the door to my elegant restaurant, gestured for him to enter, and together, he and I managed to send the crowd into hysterics. We enacted a comically flawed fifty-course meal with me playing the waiter and he playing the demanding and confused customer. At the end, and after many bursts of laughter and applause, we took a grand bow together. I opened my invisible door, and he stepped out, returning to the ordinary world and into the arms of his adoring parents.

At that moment the theatre chimes announced the start of the symphony and the audience began to make their way into the theatre to find their seats. As the boy walked away he looked back at me one last time. Our eyes met and he and I shared a deep understanding, a profound non-verbal connection that I hold dear to this day. He and I had gone somewhere together. For us, time had stood still as we lived in two worlds at once, sharing the experience with attentive witnesses. No one could take that away from us, ever. We had journeyed together to a flawless and deeply connected universe.

As I was packing up my things and collecting the money from my cleverly-decorated donation case, a man in a tux ran up to me, obviously out of breath, and said with rushed urgency, "Do you want to see the concert tonight? Our friends didn't make it, and I have an extra ticket." I accepted and took the ticket. "Excellent," he said. "You might miss the opening Ravel piece and have to watch it on the monitor, but you can enter the hall after that for the Ninth."

He dashed off and disappeared into the building. I closed my guitar case and slowly made my way to the front door. I entered the expansive lobby and checked my case full of coins at the cloak room, causing the coat check lady to giggle uncontrollably. As my ticket angel predicted, I was fated to view the Ravel piece on the lobby monitor. Then, when I and the sprinkle of other late comers were allowed into the theatre, I began to make my way toward my seat.

Picture this: I'm in my whiteface makeup and my black mime costume, trying to be inconspicuous, and yet, my seat was eighth row center. Considering where I was seated in this huge elegant hall, I could not have been more conspicuous if I'd set myself on fire. Clearly, there was no way I was going to enter unseen.

Undaunted, however, and determined to get into my seat before too many people returned from their break, I quickly walked down the side walkway to find my row. All of a sudden the whole place erupted into applause. I looked around to see what was causing this outburst and soon realized, with some shock, that this ovation was for me. People were laughing and smiling and applauding, looking at me and enjoying my surprised expression.

Honored and touched, I took an exaggerated bow and then made them laugh with my grand walk and comic stumble into my seat. The applause subsided, the lights dimmed, the curtain lifted, and before me was a spectacular orchestra and full chorus. Beethoven's Ninth symphony was magnificent and all of its stirring and elevated passages seemed exquisitely aimed at my heart.

Through my involvement in the theatre, I have been blessed with many beautiful and transcendent experiences. My two years in the mime/mask production, Mummenschanz, for example, took me to many far away places in the world, and due in part to the nature of our show and to my spiritual yearnings, I met some very remarkable people.

In Buenos Aires, I found a respected Tai Chi teacher named Felicitas, who, despite her physical handicap (after studying with her Chinese master in Argentina, the day she was to fly to China for a long-desired visit, she was hit by a truck, crippling her for life) and speaking through an interpreter, she managed to impart the essential Tai Chi form to me in record time. I took class from Ivaldo Bertozzi, the massage and Balinese dance guru in Sao Paolo, Brazil, and met with numerous accomplished puppeteers, teachers, actors, photographers, and writers of all kinds. Wherever we went, it seemed that I managed to find and bond with the most extraordinary adepts and spiritual teachers. It was an absolutely magical two years, to say the least.

However, like many of my colleagues and teachers, I became appalled at the destructive and shameful way mime became usurped by rank amateurs and talentless clowns. Too many untrained and humorless posers put on whiteface and stripes and entered the public arena to annoy the general public. Consequently, the art form enjoyed only a very short-lived blossoming before transforming, as it has so many other times in the past, into forms that could be absorbed into dance theatre, new vaudeville, clowning, and other movement arts. I, for one, am deeply grateful that I was allowed to experience the level of integrity and virtuosity that reigned during that brief window of time.

Through the years I have met and worked with some of the world's most accomplished and dedicated teachers. All of them have imparted to me much of the wisdom from their own teachers, and on and on back through time. The training and preparation opened doors for me into the worlds of stand-up comedy, stage combat, clowning, period styles, and a host of body-centered healing techniques, including the Alexander Technique, Feldenkrais, Yoga, Meditation, and scores of bio-energetic systems. I have come to know anatomy, physics, art, music, architecture, dance, literature, theatre, and psychology. And when I retired from mime as a performance tool and reentered the world of acting and directing, I found that my experiences and travels served me well.

Lest it all should appear glamorous, consider the night I sat in a chair next to the actress Maureen Stapleton at the New York Jerry Lewis Telethon. I had seen her perform onstage several times and was a great admirer of her work. Unfortunately, my presence at the telethon was as a performer from the Broadway show Mummenschanz. That meant that I was to somehow cover the phone lines for a few hours while sitting there with my toilet paper mask on my head; two rolls for eyes, two for ears, one for my nose and one for my mouth. My face was covered with a thin black hood and tucked well into a black fencing mask upon which the toilet paper features were placed. Sitting there looking ridiculous, I, nevertheless, in my excitement, turned to Maureen at my left and said, "I really love your work." She glanced up at my toilet paper features, blinked twice, and just said politely, "Thank you."

In the film, *My Dinner with Andre*, Wally Shawn, a friend of Andre Gregory and a respected man of the theatre, engages in a long and fascinating conversation about theatre, art, culture, history, and the search for what is true and good. Generally speaking, Wally's point of view supports the non-esoteric or "exoteric" life well lived, especially in the face of Andre, who had recently returned from a profound esoteric theatrical immersion with the famed Polish director, Jerzy Grotowski. At one moment in the film, Wally protests that he doesn't buy the idea that the only way to advance and evolve is through working at these "outposts" of esoteric study. Andre, on the other hand, holds the point of view that the schools, or "outposts," are the only way to progress, that the larger social structures of the world have a limited center of gravity, making it impossible to encounter the raw, unfiltered reality of the human condition and to respond to it with fresh artistry.

I suppose, as a lover of paradox, I embrace both points of view. I have seen several "outposts" and can attest to their veracity, their sincerity, and their contribution. I also feel inclined to be a warrior in the world, to experience outer and inner as part of the same thing, as part of a cosmic dream-like dance. In that way, I favor the perennial philosophy, the non-dual path of integral living. Therefore, some of this book is culled from the input of outposts and some of it comes from the more traditional exoteric avenues of learning. I leave it to you, the reader, to take what you can and to follow the hints wherever they take you.

It is my wish that this book may provide you with fresh perspectives and renewed interest in your spiritual search and your craft. I suppose I should warn you though, reading this book can be frustrating at times. Many of the chapters have metaphysical ideas that peep in and out like smiles from a derisive Cheshire cat. Add the fact, at the risk of sounding pedantic, that this book is intentionally obtuse. Why else would I use a word like obtuse? It is multifaceted and essentially granular: those deeper meanings imbedded within the text may be revealed only after concerted contemplation.

For those of you steeped already in a religious tradition or for those of you advanced in esoteric studies, whatever is familiar terrain in this book will, hopefully, be useful familiarity. For others, I can only promise that the struggle will eventually reap rewards if you simply stick with it. Like a layered piece of theatre, it will affect and hopefully inspire you upon first viewing, but with additional viewings you will find more profound connections that give real shape to the tickling hints encountered at first pass.

The traditional academic will undoubtedly be offended by the relative lack of citations and bibliographic references. How dare I assume authority and self-generate ideas or, worse, conclusions! I plead guilty. I do indeed take the liberty to state my point of view without filtering it through a cadre of like-minded fellows. In addition, much of what I impart comes from direct sources in the form of teachers whose lives and schools and influences are simply not bibliographic. What can I say? These are essays. They are meant to provoke, inspire, entertain, and hopefully, reveal something that will contribute to our collective benefit.

I remain indebted to Alan Arkin, Michael Wilson, and Ruby Allen for their kind words in support of this book, to Samuel Avital for his artistry, friendship, and guidance through the years, to E.J. Gold for his tutorials and bold Upaya stewardship, to Master Don Ahn for his eight excellences, to Maharishi Mahesh Yogi for his global optimism, to Michael Wilson once again for his loyalty through the years, to my son Ben for his continued inspiration, to Carla for her loving partnership and theatrical passion, to my many acting and directing mentors for their teachings, especially Carolyn Boone, who saw in me what I had yet to see, and to the entire family of theatre folk old and new who have carried the flame of inquiry through the darkest of ages. I extend special thanks to Iven Lourie for his many years of service to the Spiritual Path and his expert editing of this tiny piece of the puzzle.

A book, of course, cannot replace action. It is through discovering and actively working in the spiritual discipline of your choice that any of this will be of any value. Life is short and youth is often wasted on the merely curious. Get to work on yourself, set your soul in motion toward truth, toward becoming a lover of paradox, toward the causal injunction of working between two worlds.

May your efforts benefit us all.

3·10·89

E.J. Gold, *Circe,* Pen & Ink,
pencil signed, 11" x 15", Rives BFK,
© 1989 Heidelberg Editions International.

CHAPTER ONE

THE ACTOR

An actor uses the internal and external conditions of behavior to live truthfully within the imaginary circumstances of a play or filmed scenario. However, we are all actors in our lives to some degree and consequently we identify quite easily with the role-playing of professional actors. They reflect some of our own moments of high drama, great joy, trivial pursuit, deception, and triumph. They remind us that we shift roles and points of view a thousand times a day, being the hero one moment and the fool the next. Through their efforts, we peer into other cultures, other lives, other points of view, expanding our sense of the world and helping to orient and integrate our life.

Actors are essentially storytellers, exploring our collective interests, our cultural histories, and our fantasy life within an artistic framework. They tell us who we have been, who we are now, and who we might become. They are our tribal mythmakers, and in concert with writers, designers, musicians, dancers, artists, and craftsmen of all kinds, they bring stories to life. Their function and positive contribution seems obvious when seen in this perspective. Why then have they been held in such contempt throughout the ages, denied burial in Christian graves, kept out of mainstream society while at the same time celebrated, adored, and even sponsored by royalty? What is it about an actor and acting that inspires such charged contradiction? Are they more than just storytellers?

Admittedly, the stage has often been the bastion for misfits and scandalous rogues, and that, no doubt, has contributed to their disreputable image. However, that does not explain the paradoxical mix of revulsion and awe evidenced throughout history. Something more is involved in the actor's craft, some unique reference point for humans that creates this agitation. After all, the theatre in the West and in most of the world began as a sacred event, a ceremonial expression. From our vantage point today, we might see actors as individuals upon whom we have always projected our deep psychological and spiritual needs. Clearly, if we take this view, actors are more than simply storytellers.

It is important to note that even though actors began as members of an elite group of religious celebrants, especially in ancient Greece, they never achieved the degree of popularity they have enjoyed in modern times. Due largely to the global growth phenomenon of television and film, actors now enjoy a position of power and prestige never before imagined. They are admired, followed, courted, and even consulted on matters previously reserved for experts. All this for a group of folk who were often kept out of town and met with signs that read, "We do not accept Theatricals!"

The popularity of actors today, however, stands to reason. Actors are engaged in an avid search for truth, a love of research, and an uncanny ability to get results where others have failed. Indeed, their repeated exposure to the pressure of being "on" makes them prime candidates for high profile, high-pressure jobs. At this writing Arnold Schwarzenegger's latest role is as governor of California. The actor Ronald Reagan, also at one time the governor of California, went on to become president of the United States. (Maybe this says something about California!) Many actors have gone on to become directors, producers, and high paid spokespersons for charities and causes throughout the world.

Without a doubt, it's "boom-time" for actors. We could debate at length the value of this phenomenon, but we cannot ignore it. It is happening and therefore invites us to ask, "What exactly is an actor?"

We see that actors invest their energy and time in a multitude of jobs on the way to getting established. They sell products, start companies, drive taxis, wait tables, build houses, produce films, tell jokes, bartend, and anything else they can find to do en route to a successful career. So, clearly they are workers. They want and need to work. But what is it that drives them? When actors act, what is it they are doing?

Most actors do not like to talk about their craft. Rarely in interviews will an actor go into depth about the acting process. While each actor will have his or her own reasons, it is evident that they are all, like most artists, somewhat suspicious of analysis. They have worked hard to integrate their inner and outer impulses and fear that analytical scrutiny will dismantle it.

Nevertheless, on occasion, they will speak of it and sometimes they reveal much. Consider the following quotes from actors who have managed to articulate something of their craft.

"You're your first best audience long before anybody else hears you. So don't be an easy audience. Keep asking for more." –Michael Caine

"Personality is more important than beauty, but imagination is more important than both of them." – Laurette Taylor

"I really think that effective acting has to do literally with the movement of molecules." – Glenn Close

"The thing about performance, even if it's only an illusion, is that it is a celebration of the fact that we do contain within ourselves infinite possibilities." – Daniel Day Lewis

Also, thanks to a number of dedicated acting teachers and researchers, enough is known about the process to teach it and pass on the fundamentals to those people, young and old, who wish to try it. Here are some quotes from some established and influential acting teachers:

"Don't enact. Act. Don't re-create. Create. Don't imitate life. Live. Don't make graven images. Be." – Julian Beck

"…expanding one's consciousness is necessary not only in order to be affected by the impact of internal and external stimuli, but also to create the opening through which communication from the unconscious can occur."– Eric Morris

"The actor has in him the collective consciousness. It's as if all knowledge and all wisdom is contained in his mind. Through his vast imagination he inherits the wisdom of his ancestors without having had the personal experience. The actor, throughout history, has always had a deep and cosmic understanding." – Stella Adler

"Do not try to push your way through to the front ranks of your profession; do not run after distinctions and rewards; but do your utmost to find an entry into the world of beauty." – Constantin Stanislavsky

These gems of wisdom, articulated by men and women deeply involved in the craft of acting, echo the gems spoken by sages from all religious societies. They speak of truth, beauty, and the ineffable. They reveal the soulful searching that accompanies serious training in the craft. Interestingly enough, that same training parallels closely the training undertaken by aspiring students of spiritual traditions. These *chelas, sannyasins,* or "seekers" as we might call them, like the actor, must be capable of great sacrifice, must engage in considerable self-observation and reflection, must continually be tested for their dedication, and must achieve enormous powers of concentration. They both must be willing to go where the "work" is and to pursue their work out of love – not sentimental love, but love of the work itself.

In antiquity, the actor was openly linked to the spiritual paths. In Egypt, Greece, Persia, Sumeria, and in virtually all of the tribal religious cultures, the actor's work was sacred and an unquestioned contribution to the evolution of the individual and community soul. Today, that particular link is not openly addressed except in rare instances. Jerzy Grotowski, for example, the theatre director and researcher renowned for his work with the Polish Lab Theatre, held fast to a vision of the holy actor, a being he saw as capable of great physical and spiritual leaps. He and a small handful of authorities in the field have made reference to this dimension of an actor's work, and some have tried to work exclusively from that standpoint.

It has become evident to me, however, after many years delving into both the acting world and the spiritual world, that even without exposure to Grotowski or his heirs, a modern actor receives much of the same preparation a priest/priestess, shaman, or yogi receives. We can see this in certain non-psychological training methods such as the Japanese-based Suzuki method, where the formality and physical demands echo the rigors of a Buddhist boot camp. Also the more psychological methods now absorbed into mainstream acting studios reflect quite similar psychological methodologies developed by ancient monastic orders and mystery schools.

At the time of this writing, for example, there exists a popular "Big Mind" workshop taught by Zen Master Genpo Roshi. During the workshop he has the group of students shift physical postures and with each shift they are guided to assume the voice of a certain inner point of view. He has them speak as the "controller," sharing their primary point of view and then shift their posture to speak as the "skeptic," shift and speak as "vulnerable child," and shift to speak as the "protector," and so forth. In this instance, the ego in all its various defense personas is being utilized as a resource instead of destroyed or threatened. The participants are guided toward taking on various internal points of view in an exploration of the fundamental masks of the human psyche. The teacher continues in this manner, gently guiding the group out of the parade of masks and into a realization of their higher, expanded, consciousness—a level of awareness from which one is able to view all the smaller contracted sub-personas within the psyche. The various shields and masks, therefore, are honored for their existence while revealing and honoring a much larger and inclusive level of awareness.

It is a liberating experience for the Big Mind workshop participants, most of whom are interested in their spiritual evolution, and one can sense the deep satisfaction it provides. It will surprise some readers to discover that much of what is being taught in this meditation workshop is also a very typical experience for most young actors in training. The only difference is that the spiritual adept experiences the bliss of realization as related to spiritual enlightenment while the actor experiences the same bliss as related to artistic awakening. If an actor comes to know that this awakening has more than temporal value, that it is more than another booster for career aspirations, the craft becomes imbued with evolutionary import and can assume a fuller vitality.

An actor who truly wants to evolve needs to integrate the old and the new, needs to find a way to grow the various internal and external lines of talent while allowing the being component or the capital "S" Self to expand and embrace the world. In other words, a modern actor awake to the spiritual methods inherent in the craft must become a lover of paradox, must rephrase Hamlet's famous line to say: "To be and not to be, that is the answer." The new actor has the potential to transcend and include all that has gone before, and, embark upon a role that becomes truly heroic, truly imbued with star quality, truly contributing to the craft in ways that serve the truth.

However, just because the methods are present doesn't mean they are being utilized; or as the old adage goes: the secret keeps itself. It takes a strong will and sincere dedication for a modern actor to transform acting work into real spiritual work. Today's actor who is simultaneously interested in spiritual development not only must recognize the spiritual possibilities within the craft but also must choose to assume the added work that this demands. Upon encountering spiritual information, an actor must ask himself, "What is the value of this information beyond simple curiosity? Will this information enhance the craft, contribute to the body of human knowledge, and give deeper meaning to the life and work of all actors?" Like the spiritual adept, a modern actor must discover who he really is, and then he will know what needs to be done, and that will lead to doing it.

The ability for an actor to step into another reality fully and to allow his instrument to respond, free of social restraint, free of self-doubt, free of anything but the genuine flow of energy within the given circumstances of the performative event, is nearly identical to the ritual and prayerful and meditative conditions of all religious practices. The ability of an actor to differentiate her emotional and psychological components, and then re-integrate them in various configurations depicting character, is very close to the practices employed by modern and ancient monastic societies. Their aims may be different, but the process is surprisingly similar.

I have worked with actors of all ages and experience for over 25 years, and I think it is important to mention the obvious: it is possible to be a first-rate actor and even a famous and truly exceptional actor without any "spiritual" involvement whatsoever. Both worlds have so many traps for the ego that some actors are best advised to steer clear of spiritual pursuits beyond those traditional obligations supplied by their religious affiliation. Any interest in spiritual matters will only complicate their lives and might interfere with their acting progress. On the other hand, it is possible for some very unique actors to integrate both, and that is the focus of this series of essays.

Acting at its best is a non-cognitive event. That is not to say that the cognitive elements are not integrated and fully realized; they are. The actor must analyze, research, formulate clear objectives, make very specific and rational choices, and then, once the analysis is done, once the cognitive preparation and understanding is complete, the non-cognitive takes over. The actor literally plays with all the abandon, verve, integrity, and risk he can muster. There are some actors who begin as "naturals" and seem to have an innate gift for the playing and rarely rely upon the cognitive. However, to succeed and ultimately to sustain a career, they must develop reliable and very sharp cognitive skills. Some actors, on the other hand, begin with very advanced cognitive skills allowing them to discuss in detail the nuances of their character, the world of the play, the hidden themes and metaphors, but have difficulty getting out of their thoughts and into the freedom of playing. Most, of course, are a mix of the two with one or the other taking dominance, depending upon the situation.

I have devoted the greater part of my life to studying acting, training actors, and working with them in countless situations, and I am always inspired by the courage, the fortitude, and the resourcefulness of actors. Of course, there are as many types of actors as there are types of music. Some actors have very little formal training, some have tons of formal training, some are born into affluent families who are already steeped in theatrical tradition while others come from poverty. Some actors are quite neurotic and suffer greatly in their process while some sail easily through their work as if it were a walk in the park. Some actors approach their work as though it were any other job while others view it as a sacred rite with roots in ancient ritual.

What is evident to me and to many actors I know is that they gradually grow and evolve into healthy human beings because, over time, they are allowing themselves to experience being honest; both with themselves and with the world at large. They suspend restrictive moral boundaries in order to step into the psychological shadow play of honest human behavior. They get to honor and reveal what most people are forced to repress, and therefore, in the best cases, they avoid suffering from the neurosis that results from having "disowned" parts of themselves. The healthy actors claim it all. Healthy actors come to know that owning all of their humanity is the high-octane fuel for their craft and part of the formula for becoming an artist.

Many questions remain unanswered: What is the purpose of an artist? How can actors in today's marketplace find happiness and meaning in their lives? What is the ultimate aim of fully-evolved acting? What do spiritual practices have in common with the actor's artistic practices? What is going on when an actor acts?

As we begin to examine these and other topics in detail, it is important to visit briefly the threads of spiritual work woven, sometimes invisibly, into the fabric of modern acting and actor training. From this we may begin to discern what methods remain active and what methods lie dormant, awaiting renewal in this most important time. We might then awaken from the conventional flatland of the consensus point of view of acting and embark instead upon a rigorous and fulfilling process of definition that vivifies both the visible and invisible worlds.

E.J. Gold, *The Beginning,* Pen & Ink,
pencil signed, 11" x 15", Rives BFK,
© 1987 Heidelberg Editions International.

CHAPTER TWO

History and the Craft of Acting

In the West, we often mark the dawn of theatre with the advent of the ancient Greek initiation celebrations known as dithyrambs, those choral songs and dances that evolved over time into formal plays and led eventually to the highly structured play festivals. This is a convenient reference point because the Greek civilization was recent enough that we can patch together a smattering of reliable historical data from the artifacts and those few plays that have survived. It is fair to assume, however, that theatre, at least in tribal form, existed long before the Greeks developed it and indeed, long before the agrarian epoch that gave birth to city and nation states.

What format the early theatre took and to what extent those individual participants were spiritually evolved remains a mystery. Without definitive artifacts and material remnants we are left to sift through and piece together a mosaic born out of deduction, conjecture and inference. However, by observing modern, so-called "primitive" societies and the few examples of cave paintings, skeletal remains, and unearthed artifacts, we can begin to piece together information that strongly suggests that the original actor, that character who would embody the animals and invoke the spirits of the unseen world, was none other than the highly valued dancing, singing, mask-bearing tribal shaman.[1]

A shaman is a priest who, through special training and aptitude, becomes the liaison between the mysterious, invisible non-ordinary realms and the visible ordinary ones.

The shaman must master a wide spectrum of talents including the all-important ability to induce self-propelled states of ecstasy or trance.[2] His ability to voyage during trance states to other dimensions provides the shaman with very special knowledge. And because of this, he is considered by his immediate culture to have the ability to die and return to life many times during the course of his biological life-time.[3] (Hermes Trismagistus is just such a character as are many of the mythic characters described throughout ancient history.) In this way, the shaman is also the original mystic, an alchemist whose body has become a specialized alchemical furnace.

This is not to imply, however, that all actors are shamans and enter into a trance state to forge alliances with spiritual entities and shape-shift through higher or lower dimensions for the good of the tribe. They do, however, pry loose from the moorings of a crystallized psyche and come to know that the true nature of the human is as a conglomerate self, made up of many selves that function as energies interacting within the field of awareness. While most are only dimly aware of such things, some actors have experienced the profound aspects of their craft and, at least, come to appreciate the many levels involved. They are, in fact, public magicians, or shamans, hoping to tell stories by embodying them in performance conditions capable of moving our hearts, shocking loose our complacency, and bringing understanding and awareness to both subjective and objective reality.

I should mention that unless you have had direct contact with a shaman, forget what you think you know. Many people outside the shaman's culture, particularly in North America, have managed to characterize the shaman as a Hollywood-style witch doctor, branding him as a superstitious quack and a charlatan. This perception, derived no-doubt by exposure of 19th century low-level, self-described experts to equally low-level shamanic events, is quite far from the truth. Plus, very often, tribal shamans would purposely undermine their effectiveness as a way of hiding their work from unwelcome and ignorant observers. Real shamans have an elusive personality, a strong personal presence, and a strange clown-like irreverence for ordinary life. They are unpredictable in all things, yet have an uncanny and exact sense of timing, performing the appropriate gesture in ways that get results but defy codification. For some, their powers are used exclusively to heal. Others are concerned with teaching or providing spiritual guidance.

In many ways the shaman resembles the Hindu Yogi with his paranormal abilities, deep trance/meditation states, and religious authority. Yet, he differs from the classic Yogi model in that he is not turned exclusively inward, seeking enlightenment. Instead, his knowledge is outwardly oriented, directed toward serving the community.[4]

The world of the shaman is a world of expanded wisdom where consensus reality is sacrificed for the more potent non-consensus reality. As a result, en route to becoming a shaman, there are occasional bouts with what could be considered schizophrenic behavior. The shaman is trained not to become "reactive" during such episodes, which might cause premature redirection of his attention to the consensus world. Instead, he relies on an impartial attitude to the unfolding visions. This eventually brings about a positive re-integration of his psyche, allowing the shaman to re-enter the world fully engaged. In this perspective, the shaman is sometimes known as the healed madman.[5]

Both shaman and non-reductionist analysts recognize and come to know the ultimate undifferentiated mystic reality, risking madness, in order to effect sanity in service to the community. In relation to this, Levi-Strauss says:

> The shaman plays the same dual role as a psychoanalyst…Actually the shamanic cure seems to be the exact counterpart to the psycho-analytic cure, but with an inversion of all elements…psycho-analyst listens whereas the shaman speaks.[6]

Whether for healing or other purposes, shamanic invocations of spirits and trance states were, and still are, often achieved through the use of masks and dance. Masks as representatives of spirits can transport the shaman to the psychic level needed to complete his task. Dance, too, serves to induce trance, as do drum rhythms, chanting, and the ingestion of psychotropic plants.

Unlike the shaman, the modern actor, especially in America, rarely uses masks, per se, although make-up and the creation of a public persona could be considered a mask. They nonetheless use other means to invoke characters as they play "storyteller," acting out our contemporary myths and fantasies in film, television, and on the stage.

Shamans not only provide sacred functions involving the invisible realms of healing, soul navigation, dream interpretation, and so on, but they are also responsible for maintaining the tribal myths and legends through public storytelling performances.[7]   So on the one hand, we have a very serious and dedicated interior voyager and, on the other, a crazy, visionary, schizzed-out storyteller. Is this not beginning to sound more and more like the actor we all know and love today?

We can see an even clearer representation of the shamanic roots of acting in Japanese theatre. In Japan, the myths and legends are kept alive through the traditional forms of theatre, particularly the Noh theatre. In it, the actor is a purified, sanctified priest-like figure, subject to strict obligations.[8]

In addition, their belief system considers that gods are capable of inhabiting sacred objects as well as the body and character of an actor.[9] In Noh theatre, the mask and the actor are both considered sacred. When the Noh actor sits and contemplates his mask before performance, he is carrying out an ecstatic ritual that will allow the god that inhabits the mask to take full possession of him. This is in essence a shamanic technique. Shamans often use masks or objects to invoke higher or lower energies for the purpose of healing or inducing prophetic visions.

Through repeated sittings and experiences with the mask, the Noh actor opens to the invisible world. Through repeated sittings and experiences with objects, masks, rhythmic drumming, or chanting, the shaman opens to the invisible world. These repetitions are a formula of sorts, carrying both the actor and the shaman to other dimensions. For example, to ascend to the sky, he, like the shaman, *actually experiences the ascent to heavenly spheres.*[10] That is, he up-scales to another state of consciousness, activating energies appropriate to that level, radiating and performing according to the rules inherent to that level.

It appears to me that one of the major common denominators between actor and shaman seems to be the element of repetition. (I think it's interesting to note that rehearsal is a form of repetition; in fact, the French word for rehearsal is *repetition*). Through repetition of sounds, movements, and any variety of incantations, both actors and shamans surrender to the truth within another level of consciousness, giving them access to deeper and highly vivid experiences.

Chances are, this strange singing and dancing wise/fool shaman character organized rituals (repetitions), designed both to induce states of non-ordinary awareness as well as inform the tribe of his latest insight. Using this model, it is possible to consider that one specialized branch of shamanic practice, the one focused upon communal experience and group dynamics, gradually evolved and refined over the years into the source that promoted the Greek dithyrambic rituals. The knowledge, passed down through time and protected from the ignorant through special encoding practices, could very easily have been the source for rituals to invoke the gods, to celebrate key astronomical and seasonal recurrences and, as always, to provide a framework of social interaction aimed at stabilizing tribal beliefs. Soon the public and private roles of the shaman would be even more pronounced.

It seems evident to me that the public demands regarding the early worship celebrations became so great that a new class of shaman emerged to handle them, one that would specialize in these public rituals. The private shamanic practices became the province of another branch of work that remained content to exist outside the public eye. The public practice, on the other hand, grew in popularity, providing communal experiences not only to mark the seasonal changes but also to reflect upon the tragedy of war, the mysterious power of fate, the comic foibles of humans, and the profound complexities of human aspiration.

The other branch of shaman concerned itself with accessing higher states of consciousness, with voyaging deep within the psyche to discover the mysteries and the gifts of the subtle realm. It is my belief that their training and experiences, protected and hidden from public view, gave rise to the special class of shaman known as the "oracle."

The Dionysian theatre festivals were indeed popular, but Greece was also famous for its oracles. These oracles were connected to temples of the various Gods. No doubt, much of their function is lost to us in the modern age, but to a society still teetering between the magical and mythical, the advice and insight of the oracle was greatly valued. Warring kings would send their messengers to the oracle of their patron god in hopes of getting advance probabilities and possible outcomes regarding particular military campaigns.[11]

This "oracular magic" was in many ways a form of theatre using basic trance technique and simulation-magic to arrive at a suitable "reading." The temple shamans would invoke the spirits of the warring armies and then improvise a mock battle. They would then arrive at their probabilities based upon the outcome of their trance improvisation.

The oracles were used by a variety of citizens, not just kings and military advisors. They provided information to help steer the lives of anyone who came to them. Getting to them, however, was not an easy task. They were often well guarded and placed within temples that required a sojourn to find them. It took special courage and fortitude to make the journey.

For example, the messengers or "audience" would undergo a rigorous preparation before seeing the oracle at Delphi. They would often fast for three days, walk uphill several miles along a narrow path, all the while concentrating on their questions, until they reached a steam bath outpost at the base of another incline. After a purifying bath, at Castalian Spring, they would walk at night, carrying a single torch uphill along marble steps called the "Sacred Way" that led eventually to a tiny chamber, wherein they would encounter an oracular priest/priestess.[12]

Oracular ritual, then, at least at Delphi, seems to be closely aligned with private shamanic practices. The public events, like the mask, music, and dance rituals, were social rituals, occurring during celestial holidays and festivals honoring specific gods. Both esoteric and exoteric forms existed to fulfill a necessary function in the Greek world.

It is a well-known phenomenon that group energy can powerfully influence individual will. Sports arenas, funeral homes, and even comedy clubs all have their unique examples of group consciousness. It is no secret that people can be easily swept into the prevailing emotional tide of a crowd. The early Greeks capitalized on this phenomenon by provoking specific emotional reactions aimed at creating a healing unity among the audience. Motivated by desires to appease the gods, public celebrations were sometimes used to create a mass healing event known as *catharsis*. Catharsis was reached to purge the society of their collective pain and restore health and happiness to the city state.

At its zenith, with all of its discipline and innovation, the Greek theatre must have been a thrilling and profoundly moving experience for the viewing public. For Aeschylus, the first playwright, however, the desire to share insights and to reveal to the public certain discoveries led to a scandal that nearly destroyed him and almost put an end to theatre as a public event. Rarely mentioned in theatre history books is an account by Athenaeus of Naucratis stating that after his famed Orestia was produced, Aeschylus was accused of revealing secret temple rituals reserved only for the Eleusinian mystery sect of which he was a member. Apparently, this crime was punishable by death, and Aeschylus, a celebrated military general, was forced to take refuge by holding on to the altar in the temple of Dionysus for nearly three days. Authorities were forbidden to harm, kill, or remove anyone who was taking refuge at the sacred altar. Eventually, after what must have been very interesting negotiations, they agreed not to kill him as long as he agreed not to divulge any more secrets.[13]

That impulse to share sacred data, however, has remained strong through the ages. It is evidenced in many works of art and music and in the writings of William Shakespeare and several of his contemporaries. In fact, all manner of sacred data is coded into countless plays and films throughout history. Actors, therefore, wittingly or otherwise, have always been vehicles for sacred knowledge.

Related to this, I find that one event in the history of Greek theatre intrigues me above all others. It is generally understood that the theatre grew out of the religious music and dance celebrations called *dithyrambs*. It is also acknowledged that the playwright Thespis was the first actor. (Playwrights at that time were also actors in their own plays.) He was born in the 6th century in Icaria, Greece, and conceived of the idea of improving the dithyramb by stepping out from the chorus, an act that initiated the change from narrative to dramatic poetry. He also was the first to introduce the use of masks, allowing quick changes of character. Pisistratus established the first contest for tragedy in 534 B.C., and Thespis, who was by then a man of advanced years, ended up winning the top prize. His break from tradition shocked and thrilled the established order and set the stage for the development of acting and is the reason why actors, even today, are known as Thespians.[14]

Here we have the story of a man, a single human being, whose actions forever changed the shape of theatre in the Western world. Yet, we know little or nothing about what actually happened. What occurred back then that allowed for such a change, especially considering the relatively stable progression of the dithyrambic festivals for so many years?

Well, knowing what I now know, and considering the perspective of this book, I am going to throw my hat in the ring and offer a possible, albeit presumptuous, speculation. It is my belief that Thespis did not just decide one day to invent dialogue. Nor did a group of his peers or any one maestro coerce him into such a fundamentally revolutionary act. I believe that he transcended the chorus; that through accident or device, he refined his nervous system to the degree that, much like a shaman in trance, he was guided to introduce a new, singular voice separate from the chorus.

Keep in mind that inner guidance of this magnitude has always been viewed with suspicion and mistrust. In fact, the Greek philosopher Socrates attributed much of his knowledge to the "voices" that counseled him regularly.[15] Also, it is relatively common knowledge that nearly all composers, poets, artists, writers, inventors, and the like confess to feeling guidance of some kind or another. Certain people, however, become the embodied vocal conduit for direct contact with the beyond—a mouthpiece for the subtle realm, so to speak. These people are capable of suspending their personal identities in order to allow other ones to take voice. They are more controversial from time to time, because of the disorienting theatrical effect of transmitting direct signals from the spirit world. But the fact is, all of us, especially actors, are receivers, isotopes of one kind or another. There are countless tales of performers reaching extraordinary heights during a performance, and then later feeling amazed and humbled; feeling as though the performance came through them, not from them.

In actuality, we all experience glimpses of channeling every day. It comes as a "hunch," or hearing a song on the radio that seems to speak directly to you, or secret beliefs in lucky charms, self-coaching before a stressful event, message-filled dreams, getting the sudden urge to call a friend, and so forth.

One might argue that these are just the activities of the subconscious mind at work. Yes, but that unfortunate word, subconscious, should not be relegated to the lower order simply because of the prefix, "sub." That part of our consciousness is vast primal territory, just beginning to be explored by science. And anyway, why should a primal or pre-conscious state of awareness preclude highly sensitive receiving and transmitting powers?

Ordinarily, we habitually ignore the more subtle activities of our awareness in favor of the agreed upon hard-edged "real" world. Not so the artist and certainly not so the actor. A serious actor in training begins early on to observe every nuance of self in an effort to bring it more into the sphere of conscious direction. The effort to achieve this is the same effort and mechanism employed by psychics as they adjust internal mood, intent, powerful listening, and the courage to doubt consensus notions of reality.

It seems evident to me that prophets, holy men, sages, alchemists, shamans, inventors, and even some scientists know what the Vedas have been saying all along: that *all knowledge is structured in consciousness.* Mastering the structure and accessing the variety of frequencies in the band of human consciousness is the work of all artists. Actors, too, share this adventure and they have done so all along.

Sadly, the majority of humans on earth find the notion of other dimensions, voices, and higher consciousness either above or beneath their concerns. They content themselves with purely material pursuits.

That would be fine if that were all they did. Too often, however, these people have compulsive reactions against anyone whose ambitions run deeper than the accumulation of earthly power. Typically this manifests as fear, which soon translates into anger, defense, and aggression. This behavior is not unlike the college roommate who begins to display contempt and even active aggression towards the other roommate who chooses to study and devote herself to the learning process.

Therefore, throughout history, those people wanting to reach their highest potential and avoid distraction in the form of persecution, often joined together in groups, forming schools and brotherhoods. Most monasteries and nunneries of all faiths were established for these and related reasons.

Schools in one form or another have flourished nearly everywhere in the world: in Egypt, in the highlands of Tibet, in the Caucasus mountains of Georgia, in the caves of Greece, and in the deserts of Persia, to name a few. Anyone who saw Peter Brook's film or read the book *Meetings With Remarkable Men* by G.I. Gurdjieff, has a good idea of what is considered a school.

At these schools, then as now, certain laws were revealed and tested. These laws, which usually established experimental connections with mathematical law, natural order, and human possibility, were carefully guarded. In the Pythagorean schools, for example, novices had to undergo a five-year vow of silence before entering the serious phase of study.[16]

During specific intervals, however, the schools would reveal to the outside world portions of their discoveries. Pythagoras, for example, is credited with a number of major gifts to mankind, including the invention of the Western musical scale, the laws governing certain geometrical shapes, as well as theories about the movements of the planets and the stars and the transmigration of souls.[17]

When these discoveries were made public, it had to be done with great caution. In many cases the discoveries from schools shattered old world concepts and often radically changed man's existence. Therefore, like people carrying bright lights, the schools were careful not to shine them all at once, for fear of blinding or confusing those people accustomed to the dark.

Perhaps the Thespis event was one such revelation. Or perhaps it was a sudden and unplanned psychic phenomenon. Maybe it was a lucky "accident" that seemed to work so, being a practical man of the theatre, he kept it. Or maybe not. Maybe Thespis is a story created to explain the existence of dramatic structure. Perhaps the existing mystery schools never had contact with the theatre, and the plays enacted there had no relationship with the schools whatsoever. Yet, considering the priest-like roles of the actors at the time and the daring concepts exposed in Greek drama, I am inclined to believe that the mystery schools were at least partially involved in the work of the stage,

With the domination of the Roman Empire, theatre was forced to serve the rough and popular demands of the day, quickly devolving into promotional extravaganzas for the Church. Greece, too, had its share of what Peter Brook calls the "rough theatre,"[18] but it was always balanced with a holy tradition. Roman rule, however, destroyed all that. What then happened to the mystery schools and the impulse toward holy theatre during this time?

The answer is they went underground as much true art does in times of political unrest and occupation. Later, as the empire began to crumble, and as the new Christian force began to take hold, actors were either absorbed into the rituals of the church, or forced to band together in small gypsy-like troupes.

The traveling troupes of Europe had the advantage of contact with people and ideas from other lands. It's conceivable that they could have formed links with other mystery schools from Byzantium or the Far East.

But any knowledge outside the sanctions of the ever more powerful Church was considered heresy and was surely a dangerous preoccupation at the time. Therefore, certain laws and discoveries had to be hidden or "occluded" to insure protection against the Church. It is even possible that the lamps of cosmic law and the knowledge of man's spiritual destiny were kept safe by being coded into acrobatic and juggling shows of the time. (I know for a fact that not a few contemporary shows of similar type are outgrowths or, at least, closely allied to the work of mystery school activities.)

These gypsies continued to develop their secret wisdom of herbs, divination and fertility, while maintaining their living through magic shows, minstrel parades, and comic playlets. These nomadic characters have had many names but are generally known to historians as *jongleurs.*[19]

The popular Italian *jongleurs* maintained a family tradition of theatre and stayed together for generations, entertaining throughout Italy and abroad. Among other things, they presented clever scenarios using a collection of recurring stock characters (not unlike popular animated cartoons such as The Simpsons). The style came to be known as Commedia Del' Arte and it showcased the characters of *Arrlechino, Puchinello, Dottore, Pedrolino, Colombina,* and so on. The fact that these characters were such strong archetypes suggests that some Italian players had access to the mystery school data on human typicalities.

This law is basic to nearly all mystic traditions with slight variances from culture to culture. Quite simply, it is based on the premise that humans are all formed from a prescribed set of types with each type having a specific energy composition and life function. Some contemporary schools rely on the astrological model for this, others on the psychological post-Jungian models. I have found the best beginning model of the law of typicalities to be in Don Richard Riso's book, *Personality Types–Using the Enneagram for Self–Discovery.*

The Russian counterparts to the Italian players, known as *skomorokhi* (minstrels), also lived under the domination of the Church. They had previously been priests who presided over many cyclic festivals and used their magical powers to heal, divine future events, and maintain ritual songs and incantations. Under Christian rule, however, their works were limited to theatrical amusements including improvised comic dialogues, puppetry, and the famous dancing bear acts.[20]

I have no doubt that the reason actor/priests in countries under Church rule were disempowered and shunned by the Christian leaders was not just because they worshipped "pagan" gods. I have a hunch they could put on a pretty hilarious and irreverent Saturday Night Satire, mocking the pomposities of the local clergy. And since reverence was mandatory and necessary for the installation of the new order, it was "hit the road" time for satirical and disrespectful minstrels.

Theatre, like nearly everything else, suffered the chaos of the Dark Ages. In the tenth century, however, it emerged in an organized form: giving voice to brief biblical plays. These liturgical works were allegories enacted by the various craftsmen, community members belonging to one of the many guilds. The guilds were given permission and support by the Church to meet the communal need for theatre.

The rituals, which proved to be a useful teaching tool for the Church since so much of the population was illiterate, continued to grow in popularity. They soon became large festivals designed to help celebrate holy days such as Easter. These progressed into full-scale pageant plays with multiple settings and a wide number of theatrical effects.

Keep in mind that within the liturgy of the Church itself, many of the essential elements of theatre were still at work in full force: the ritual of mass, the acoustical ambiance of a cathedral, focus-directing architecture, flickering red candles with a splash of color from stained glass windows on a marble floor, not to mention the chanting of nuns and monks, all combining to create a theatrical and highly dramatic spectacle that rivaled the mosques and temples of Persia.

And the mystery schools? In most of Europe, non-Christian mystery schools went deep underground, living in fear of the Catholic armies. Many of them enacted false conversions or retreated to obscurity in the south of France. The Cathars were slaughtered as heretics. Christian mystery schools, on the other hand, in the shape of monastic orders flourished. And things stayed pretty much the same for generations until the Renaissance.

Formal theatre, which had blended symbiotically with the Church, soon asserted its independence. It moved swiftly through Tudor drama, improving all the while, until it managed to reach its finest moment during the late Elizabethan period with the unparalleled genius of William Shakespeare.

Shakespeare's work still looms as the outstanding example of theatre that is at once elite and elevated while also being popular and rough. His plays manage to cross nearly all barriers of class and gender as well as time and space, fulfilling their royal and popular mission to inspire and entertain for four centuries. It is a feat of artistic achievement that matches any of the other great accomplishments of the Renaissance. In fact, his plays are so numerous, the language so full, the plots so different, that some scholars have entertained the notion that they were not written by him at all. They contend that because of the lowly status awarded a playwright at the time, other poets actually wrote the plays, but conspired to pin the credit on an actor named William.

The "conspiracy" theory remains unresolved to this day, due to the fact that British authorities refuse to exhume Shakespeare's remains (a fact supporters of the conspiracy theory see as evidence for their case). Regardless of who wrote them, and considering the evidence supporting his existence, I have no problem accepting William Shakespeare as the true and proper author of the plays. The simple and undeniable fact is that they exist and actors have performed them for centuries.

Shakespeare's plays remain popular because they are full of mystical elements that reflect the vigorous exercise of free-thinking of the day. *Hamlet*, *A Midsummer Night's Dream*, *The Tempest*, *King Lear*, *Macbeth*, and many others approach subjects considered heretical in the not-too-distant past. The Ghost of Hamlet's father visiting him, for example, or the Druidic and magical playfulness of Oberon and Titania's woodland world, the conjuring witches in *Macbeth*, the recurring references to astrological fatalism in *Romeo and Juliet*, *Cymbelene*, and many more, all display the new freedoms enjoyed by the theatre of the day.

Yet, at the same time, there arose a strong reaction against such freedom. The reaction took the shape of religious persecution against the Neo-Platonist movement and anyone caught delving into the mystical arts without strict sanctions from the Church. In 1600, Giordio Bruno, for example, was burned at the stake for his interests in Egyptian magic, as a symbolic warning to others.[21]

Not surprisingly, under such heated conditions, many of the free thinkers of the day retreated to the relative sanctuary of secret societies. These were newly-adopted mystery schools, many of which maintained strong links to the ancient lineages.

John Dee, the popular scientist, Queen Elizabeth's philosopher, the founder of the Rosicrucian Order, and one of the most celebrated men of the Elizabethan age, came under attack for his interests in "occult" philosophies. One such attack came in dramatic form when Christopher Marlowe presented his play *Doctor Faustus*. The play presented a rather seedy portrait of a conjurer who sells his soul to Lucifer, but repents unsuccessfully at the hour of his death. The play was an obvious attempt to disgrace Dee by insinuating that he and others like him were malevolently conjuring devils.[22]

Shakespeare, who wrote of witches, faeries, and demons, must have come under careful scrutiny at the time as well. Perhaps it was due to his popularity—or to the fact that theatricals were considered damned anyway—that he never endured the kind of public defamation John Dee had to withstand. Of course, Shakespeare merely wrote about such things, he never openly admitted to delving into them as John Dee had done.

Nevertheless, during the latter period of his writing and while still enjoying the sponsorship and patronage of the highest authority in the land, who at this time was none other than King James himself, Shakespeare created *The Tempest*. In it, Prospero, the main character, is openly a conjurer. The difference is his magic is "white" magic, used for utopian ends and therefore sanctioned by the court. Aside from being a wonderful play and a popular hit, his play also did much to cool the witch-hunt frenzy that had gripped the country and helped establish white Cabala as legitimate. And in many ways it helped to vindicate John Dee, who had fallen from a position of prominence to obscurity and poverty.[23]

As the Restoration era settled in and the theatre of manners took over, the spiritual dimensions of acting waned considerably. It was later to resurface with a vengeance in the work of Ibsen, Strindberg, Yeats, Artaud, and many others involved in the realist, symbolist, and surrealist movements of the late 19th and early 20th centuries.[24]

These movements gave rise to the next wave of playwrights and men of the theatre whose work resonates and informs nearly all of contemporary drama. Chief among them are Ionesco, Meyerhold, Beckett,

Pirandello, Brecht, Grotowski, and Stanislavski.

Ionesco penetrated into our collective reactions to light and shadow. He also forced us to hear our own mad laughter as we come face to face with the modern cycle of acceleration, proliferation, and destruction.

Meyerhold attempted to demystify acting by creating a new set of training tools called *biomechanics*. With it, he introduced the notion of the actor's body as an athletic, ultimately acrobatic instrument, capable of responding to theatrical situations with total non-linear commitment.

Beckett gave us the power of his singular gift for the theatrical metaphor. His *Waiting for Godot* will most probably live on as the greatest dramatic masterpiece of the 20th century.

Brecht opened our eyes to the neurosis and mass hypnosis involved in the "suspension of disbelief," that tacit understanding of the audience to allow themselves to believe in the action of a play or film. He strove to cleanse the eye and mind of its dreamy habit of falling into a play the way one falls into a book. He envisioned theatre as an agitprop tool and developed a new aesthetic derived from his need to remove all traces of the hypnosis that influenced the art, theatre, music, and literature of the day.

Grotowski, in an effort to center his work on the essential and spiritual, shed all previous notions of acting and began a true laboratory of investigation where the soul of the actor took precedence over any other element.

The absurdity of Ionesco, the playful formalism of Meyerhold, the holy dread of Beckett, the astringent sting of Brecht, and the ritual courage of Grotowski all contributed in their own way to the growth and vitality of twentieth century theatre.

It is Constantine Stanislavski's work, however, that I find to be the most profoundly influential for the Western actor, particularly in terms of spiritual advancement. This might seem odd at first, especially considering the extent to which his work has been associated with what is typically considered to be non-spiritual realism. But the more I delved, the more I realized that he had been using, consciously or unconsciously, some important mystery school ideas. These ideas were, and still are, powerful tools used in spiritual training. Some of these techniques shared between these two quite separate worlds I shall describe in later chapters.

That brings us, with no claim of exhaustive analysis, to the contemporary scene. Actors today are working in all media and in all countries. The explosion of work is fantastic, and it has extended to many non-western countries such as South Korea and India. It is amazing that the work of this one man, a Russian with a passion for acting, would end up having such a global influence. All over the world actors are still being trained with numerous variations on Stanislavski's original work.

It is fascinating to me to observe that with only a slight shift in emphasis and approach, much of actor training becomes spiritual training. With a shift of perspective, all of the great contributors previously mentioned could be integrated into a new whole, filtered through Stanislavski's systematic approach and guided by a super objective aimed at spiritual work.

What do I mean by *spiritual* work? Well, virtually all religious sources suggest that we are here to prepare for a form of graduation. Each religion has its own curriculum, so to speak, with the hierarchy of development, suggesting grades or levels. Most world religions adhere to the notion of reincarnation: cycles of return visits until we are beyond the need for human experiences. Christianity and certain other religions adhere to the one-shot idea: you make it this time or not at all. Regardless of the belief system, they all function within the same model: *steps taken in this lifetime, moving to an ultimate non-material goal.*

Each religion has its own way of describing this goal and its own unique yardstick to measure progress along the way. Most often progress in a religion is measured by the appraisal of an elder or a group of peers who are somewhere further up the ladder. What unites them, however, is that as the new spiritual awareness takes root, the adepts usually speak of feeling closer to God; they take more responsibility for their actions and exhibit remarkable personal fortitude, fearlessness, compassion, purposefulness, and striking individuality.

In my opinion, the aim of all spiritual work boils down to two basic results. One group wishes for redemption, a kind of graduation from earth forged through grace or faith or good works, resulting after death in acceptance into a blissful and peaceful place often known as Heaven; a place where they hope to live for eternity. The other group hopes to awaken to their higher Self and have the kind of experience that frees them from fear of death enabling them carefully to apply their knowledge consciously to return to this plane of existence in order to help others to do the same. Some in this latter category assume the added responsibility of awakening the creator who, by the misuse of man's free will, has fallen asleep into his own creation.[25]

Pretty heady stuff—and not normally the province of the theatre. In today's world, an actor's aim is usually more aligned with the worldly pursuit of "making it." This general idea of success is a little different for each person, but it usually involves limousines, autographs, and lots of quality roles to play well into old age. While I encourage all actors to pursue their dreams, I am compelled to ask, "What is the purpose of making it?" When all is said and done, when all the hunger for approval and love and the desire for money and attention is played out, the spiritual dimension still calls as the one thing that can provide a sense of real purpose.

Keep in mind, the spiritual dimension of acting is not for everyone. It is only for those few souls who hunger for a deeper calling, need to serve a purpose higher than their personal concerns, and who are committed to transformative theatre that awakens without pandering to marketplace trends. Most actors have been conditioned to see that kind of sacred life-aim as foreign to the art of theatre. Fortunately, that perception is rapidly changing.

It is apparent to me and to a growing number of artists and educators, that throughout history there has been a thread of spiritual influence weaving itself into every facet of life, including the craft of acting. Let us recognize this and assume responsibility for nurturing its growth. And given the vast influence of actors in the world today, it strikes me as an ideal time to define an integral approach to the art. Perhaps the modern actor's adventure toward real enlightenment can cut through the noise and give leverage toward a positive outcome for humanity and all sentient life. What better role to play than that?

E.J. Gold, *Mystic Realist,* Pen & Ink,
pencil signed, 11" x 15", Rives BFK,
© 1986 Heidelberg Editions International.

CHAPTER THREE

THE MYSTIC REALIST?

In his autobiography, *My Life in Art*, Constantin Stanislavski gives us a candid look at his family life in Moscow and the events which formed his interest in the theatre. By all accounts, he was a normal young boy, a bit privileged perhaps, not all families can afford to build a small stage on which their kids can play, but normal nonetheless. What thrilled him the most was being allowed to go with his father to see the Opera.

After witnessing a number of performances that moved him deeply, he began to focus his energy towards his new-found desire: to be an actor. His father, thinking it was a passing phase, gave him free reign to entertain his fantasies, at least until he was of age. At that time he was expected to join the family business.

As is often the case with adolescents, Constantin had other plans. He felt compelled to try his hand at acting. Knowing he would displease his father and not wanting his family to risk public ridicule if he failed, Constantin changed his name from Alexiev, which was his real name, to Stanislavski, his chosen stage name. His father, however, soon found out about his performing experiences and was no doubt greatly displeased. Yet, there was nothing he could do, it was too late, Constantin was officially hooked.

Luckily for Stanislavski, who at first was not a very good actor, wealth and life circumstances allowed him the luxury of dabbling in the theatre long enough to establish himself as a fairly competent actor. He learned the old fashioned way, through trial and error and emulating the accomplished actors he admired. Later in life, after much struggle and near continuous work on himself and his craft, he was considered a masterful actor, admired by all who saw him perform.

There were a growing number of accomplished actors in Russia and Europe at the time, but what is remarkable about Stanislavski is that he went beyond that. He chose to uncover the underlying conditions that lead to artistic inspiration. During his search, he quickly realized that there was no reliable process of training the actor. No one seemed to have a clear idea of how an inspired moment occurred and why it was so fleeting. Everything was left, more or less, to chance. He could not tolerate this unnecessary condition and devoted his life to the consistent investigation of what a person can do to be a truly great actor. And as a result of his efforts, actors now have reliable methods of preparing themselves for the stage and screen.

Stanislavski was trying to understand the invisible forces that help an actor enter imaginary worlds, take on other manifestations, realize vivid relationships, and move the depths of the viewer's soul. When you start down this road in earnest, delving into invisible forces, you sooner or later come upon ideas and practices that are in alignment with mystery school discoveries. A true inner search leads inevitably and quite naturally to those ideas and exercises that have been the standard for mystics and shamans for centuries. For example, one of the basic and most pervasive beginning training tools in nearly all spiritual disciplines is activating comprehensive self-observation. In fact, the Russian mystic Gurdjieff used this technique almost exclusively as he labored to endow people with the power of self-remembering:

> Knowledge of oneself is a very big, but a very vague and distant aim... Self-study is the work or the way which leads to self-knowledge. But in order to study oneself one must first learn how to study, where to begin, what methods to use .... The chief method of self-study is self-observation. Without properly applied self-observation a man will never understand the connection and the correlation between the various functions of his machine [body], will never understand how and why on each separate occasion everything in him 'happens.'[1]

Compare that with what Stanislavski states: "If you only knew how important is the process of self-study! It should continue ceaselessly, without the actor even being aware of it, and it should test every step he takes."[2]

Nearly all approaches to acting give at least some attention to powers of observation and self-study. This is because, quite obviously, the actor must know his own manifestations before attempting to harness them for theatrical use.

The prerequisite for advanced powers of observation is concentration. Highly-developed powers of concentration can be seen in many endeavors, from martial arts to the prayers of a Trappist monk. Of course, certain activities utilize different aspects of this power. A race car driver must have a particularly sharp form of concentration while driving at speeds in excess of 200 miles per hour. The sculptor, on the other hand, must demonstrate a longer span of concentration of quality exactly suited to the material he is shaping.

A number of religious disciplines are notable for their unusual dedication to the power of concentration. Zen Buddhism, for example, is famous for its rigorous concentration, especially as it applies to meditation. And there is a Sufi technique designed to expand or contract the field of awareness by diffusing the vision and not following any particular thing, even in a busy marketplace. Hindu and Tibetan monks will often spend long hours concentrating on a painting or a candle flame. Catholics pray the rosary and Quakers sit in peaceful silence.

And actors? Here is what Stanislavski says about *concentration* as it relates to the work of the actor:

> If you gave a man a magic mirror in which he could see his thoughts, he would realize that he was walking about on a heap of broken pieces of his begun, unfinished and abandoned thoughts. Just like a shipwrecked vessel: pieces of torn velvet material, bits of broken masts...and every sort of flotsam and jetsam.
>
> This is what thoughts of a beginner in the studio, who can neither concentrate his attention, nor keep it fixed on one object, are like.
>
> And so we have come to the first step of the creative art of the state, a step that is unalterable and common to all—concentration of attention, or to put it more briefly, concentration.[3]

And:

> ... In mastering it and in learning to concentrate all the powers of your organism on some particular part of it, you learn at the same time the art of transforming your thought into, as it were, a fiery ball. Your thought, strengthened by your attention and put into words, in a definite rhythm will, provided it is spoken by you in a state of full concentration, break through all the unconventional stage situations you may have to deal with, and find its way straight to the heart of the spectator.[4]

Stanislavski introduced the use of circles of concentration to train his actors. In this technique, the actor expands his or her concentration in an ever-widening circle, as far as can be sustained; when the circle begins to waver it must withdraw to a smaller radius which can be easily sustained by visual attention. Gifted actors can maintain several circles at once—monitoring the stage picture and the attention of the audience while sustaining laser-sharp focus in a specific unit of action.

Stage presence, that magnetic quality in some actors, seems to be a by-product of a powerfully expanded circle of concentration. In my experience, it is the result of expanding a circle to include the entire audience, while simultaneously maintaining very focused and detailed onstage circles.

Obviously film actors must utilize their circles of concentration differently. To insure that their subtle camera reality is small enough, yet potent enough to captivate the viewer, they must hold a tight circle that is just wide enough to include the camera. And of course, all good actors instinctively manipulate their focus of attention with clarity and discrimination.

Once concentration is established and self-observation begins to occur, actors, like adepts, must next begin to understand the division of functions in the instrument. There is a movement center that can be trained and integrated through the study of mime, dance, stage combat, postural alignment techniques, yoga, tai chi, and so forth. There is a thinking center that can be trained through research, script analysis, and line memorization. There is an emotional or feeling function that can be accessed through breath, relaxation, and imagination. There is a vocal function that relies upon mastering breath and articulation, the clear healthy use of the vocal resonators, all of which can be trained through the various voice methodologies developed by the great vocal teachers such as Linklater, Lessac, Rosenberg, Fitzmaurice, and numerous others. And finally, there is a little understood integrating function that I have called the "intentionality" function. This function is the activation of will with the simultaneous ability to surrender to the imaginary circumstances. It is a part of the instrument that requires great courage and the capacity to withstand the barrage of distortion factors that accompany the actor's journey.

In addition, it is important to recognize that every actor has a different chemistry and was born with an instrument that is composed of a certain configuration of the aforementioned functions. This means that each person will have a different reaction to the same stimulus; he or she will process it differently. How they process it is governed in part by the *type* of person they are. All actors, like all people, have a center of gravity from which they lead into the world. One area along the spectrum of their personality can be counted upon to predominate.

When actors begin to understand what type of people they are and how they are uniquely conditioned to view the world, they can then begin to reprogram their instruments, taking them into territories outside their types.

In advanced work, the actor/adept can reprogram the instrument for a specific aim. An actor, for example, may wish to create a character that is radically different from his personal configuration. The spiritual adept may wish to overcome habitual mind patterns and simply open his heart to God. The initial step, before any of this happens for actors and adepts alike, is to arrive at an impartial state, a balanced, unbiased, a-moral (not immoral) place of objectivity, whereby their choices can range very far without fear of losing themselves.

In India, the system most employed for this purpose is the balancing of the energy centers commonly called the "chakras." Chakras are seven basic energy centers that correspond to certain glands in the body. There is a lot of research and written material concerning the chakras, so it is not necessary to go into detail here. I will, however, give the location of the centers and their corresponding glands.

The first chakra is located at the base of the spine and corresponds to the adrenals, the second is located in the center of the pubic bone and relates to the sexual glands, the third is located at the navel and relates to the spleen, the fourth is located just below the sternum at the solar plexus, the fifth is located at the throat in the nook where the clavicle bones meet and it relates to the thyroid, the sixth is located in the lower forehead between the eyebrows and corresponds to the pituitary gland, and the seventh and final chakra is located at the center of the top of the head, corresponding to the pineal gland.[5]

There is, of course, the gross level body that we all can see and experience readily as the skeletal system, the muscle system, the cardio vascular system, the neurological system, the lymphatic system, the viscera, and so forth. However, the composition of the human being does not stop there. Woven into that already quite complex and amazing structure there is a set of systems that are invisible yet both accessible and sophisticated.

The energy centers that make up the chakra system, recognized and understood for many centuries in India, are components of the energy system of the body. They are part of a much larger network of energy lines that comprise what is sometimes called the subtle body. This energy network is composed of thousands of tiny nadis or energy points, the same ones utilized by acupuncturists to help manage pain and heal the body.

The chakra system processes vital energy from the air called "prana" and uses it to stimulate the various centers, achieving a variety of results. Regarding the chakra system, Stanislavski states:

> I have read what the Hindus say on this subject. They believe in the existence of a kind of vital energy called Prana, which gives life to our body. According to their calculation, the radiating center of this Prana is the solar plexus. Consequently, in addition to our brain which is generally accepted as the nerve center and psychic center of our being, we have a similar source near the heart, in the solar plexus....[6]

Now, of course, the Indian system is much more exact than what Stanislavski describes (he mentions only the *Manipura* chakra at the solar plexus, which the Hindus view as the *will center*—the spiritual vortex of free will), but he does give the fundamental basis for contacting the powerful energies needed for powerful acting. He further relates his personal use of the chakra idea in achieving a link between the mental and the emotional center, resulting in the ability to "commune with myself onstage either audibly or in silence, and in perfect self-possession."[7] While not exactly an expert in spiritual disciplines, his motives were clear: searching for means to secure excellence in acting.

Yet, how wonderful to know that he came to formulate his own experiments by borrowing at times from the spiritual techniques of the Hindus. It's even more wonderful when one realizes that modern actors, especially in the mid-twentieth century, in an attempt to be *avant-garde* and break new ground, adopted elements of Hindu spiritual disciplines. Stanislavski had beaten them to it by several decades!

Stanislavski also inspired many American teachers of acting, Lee Strasberg, Stella Adler, and Sanford Meisner, to name a few. They were a part of the famed "Group Theatre" that formed in the late 1930's in New York City. They took their inspiration from Stanislavski and began to experiment with his ideas, guiding a whole new generation of actors that hit the scene with great power and potency. Yet, for all the advancements and depth, there was a price.

The Freudian aspects of Strasberg's work gave his actors a mysterious power to summon emotions from their depths. As Freud discovered, there are certain memories stored in the conscious and subconscious mind that can be re-visited. An actor might choose to harken back to a certain memory that holds an emotional charge, and upon contact with the memory, the actor's nervous system begins to re-experience it as if it were real. In this way the actor could manifest very convincing emotional states that would serve to energize and inform the acting work.

Exciting and liberating at first, this experiment later proved to have a high unreliability factor. One theory for its failure was that, like certain pieces of music that move us, after repeated hearings the effect becomes less and less until we are no longer moved as we once were. Actors were forced to keep digging into their pasts to find more and more emotional well-springs, and over time there emerged evidence that this process was creating actors who were increasingly self-absorbed and under-prepared for anything but gritty realism or cinematic naturalism. The attention given to "emotional recall" became controversial and seemed to invite a self-indulgence at best and neurotic tendencies at worst.

Stella Adler had a more expansive process of working, providing discipline and theatricality and a technique that added renewed interest in mastering classical works while still encouraging a deeply personal approach.

Sanford Meisner, who taught for many years at New York's Neighborhood Playhouse, responded in his own way to this growing problem among the new breed of actors by developing a methodology that used what was useful about Stanislavski's early experiments, but went on to include more of his later experiments dealing with the theory of "Actions."

He saw that one of the problems with all beginning actors is that they were allowing their intellect to get in the way. They were conceiving of the role in their heads and then pretending to pretend. This caused all manner of artificiality and false sentimental emotionalism that had nothing at all to do with the unfolding reality on stage.

Meisner, like Stanislavski, saw that acting was not "feeling" but was instead "doing" and his integrity regarding this view became his greatest gift to modern acting.

With the emphasis on doing, Meisner's approach helps actors to develop a way of working that takes their usual self-centered, self-absorbed, and self-monitoring energy and turn it around to become more fully invested in the "other." All necessary emotional preparation was trained to be activated by use of the imagination, steering away from actual recollections, and was only utilized as a way of filling the actor with the essential problem of the character. Then, unlike previous methods, the actor would not "play the problem," but instead would do the behavioral work needed to effect change in the other character in order to solve the problem.

This simple idea, whereby the actor's attention flows outward toward fulfilling a defined action while being absolutely available to the partner or partners in any given scene, has proven over time to be a remarkably healthy and remarkably reliable development. When an actor finally releases self-obsession, surrenders any conceptual interference with the unfolding action, and when all of the acting is a matter of spontaneously reacting to stimulus, the usual narcissistic tendencies recede. The actor, in essence, recognizes the other as the source of his or her artistic inspiration, and gradually, with practice, a deep, relaxed, and completely alive presence emerges.

Actors working in this way cease to exist as this bundle of emotional agendas and instead become acted upon, responding honestly and living truthfully under imaginary circumstances. It is as if a powerful, more vivid reality is being newly minted moment-by-moment; effortless and perfectly timed. It is, in fact, very close, if not identical, to the ideal state of awareness often associated with Zen Buddhism.

In addition to self-observation, concentration, activation of powerful energy centers, and learning the ability to live truthfully under imaginary circumstances, Stanislavski recognized that tension was the enemy of artistic expression. Nearly everyone who speaks in public recognizes that excess tension reduces breath capacity and vocal range. But the most destructive aspect of excess tension in acting, and in spiritual work, is the fact that tension hinders access to the subconscious.

This limitation is one reason why Yoga masters, Tai Chi teachers, and spiritual counselors of all kinds encourage relaxation. Relaxing the mind and body allows freedom of circulation, a calmer, clearer state of mind that in turn allows a greater appreciation for the subtler energies of the body.   Sounding very much like a classical Tai Chi teacher, Stanislavski says:

> Madame Sonora has drawn your physical attention to the movement of energy along a network of muscles. This same kind of attention should be fixed on ferreting out points of pressure in the process of relaxing our muscles – a subject we have already considered in detail. What is muscular pressure or a spasm except moving energy that is blocked?
>
> From your experiences last year in the sending out of certain rays or wordless communications, you know the energy operates not only inside us but outside as well; it wells up from the depths of our beings and is directed to an object outside ourselves.
>
> It is important that your attention move in constant company with the current of energy, because this helps to create an endless, unbroken line which is so essential to our art. [8]

And:

> ... therefore, be quite bold in throwing off as much tension as you possibly can. You needn't think for a moment that you will have less tension than you need. No matter how much you reduce tension, it will never be enough...Your own physical and spiritual truth will tell you what is right. You will sense what is true and normal better when you reach the state that we call, *I am*. [9]

The flow of energy and the active sending out of rays is the conscious utilization of the etheric body in man.   In Taoist terms he is referring to the flow of "chi" in the body along the meridians that flow unobstructed in a relaxed person who has refined his nervous system. Not only does Stanislavski imply that courage is needed, in his words to, "throw off tension," but also he clearly states that it will be rewarded with a particular state of awareness called "I am." This is amazing to me because this "I am" is the state of graceful presence referred to in exactly the same way by Buddhists, Sufis, Kabbalists, Christians—virtually all religions.

A Kabbalist teacher and friend of mine told me not long ago that according to his tradition, the problem with humanity is the addition of an object. He explained that scripturally, "I am" is divine. But man felt compelled to include more, making phrases like these: I am angry, or I am an American, or I am a mechanic. As you see, division and confusion begins with the inclusion of one extra word, one layer of self-identification.

Clearly, an actor can't walk out on stage and play "I am" and hope to tell the story effectively. Just creating a state of being is too passive and goes against the very nature of acting, which as we have established is "doing." Instead, Stanislavski's injunction seems to point toward arriving at an impartial state of awareness from which the sense of what is true becomes more accurate or more vivid. One does not place emphasis on one state against the other, but embraces all states as a by-product of this impartiality.

It is evident to me that spiritual work and certain acting techniques developed by Stanislavski intersect and share common elements that are working towards common goals. Both realms work on self-observation, impartiality, knowledge of the energy centers of the body, relaxation, presence, discernment of what is true, and a balanced state of dedication to something higher than oneself—be it God, the Absolute, Jesus, Art, or whatever name we give it.

And above all, it is amazing to know that the state of grace recognized by most religions as "I am" is also held by Stanislavski, the father of modern acting, as a valuable goal for developing actors.

Much of what has been established in American acting owes its existence to this Russian, who for too many years has been strictly identified as the vanguard of realism. The Actor's Studio and other such offshoots did indeed refine and Americanize his concepts; but only enough to feed the increasing demand for cinematic reality. What of our deeper, spiritual realities?

It is time to re-evaluate the course of acting today, to reinvigorate the spiritual impulses behind Stanislavski's life's work. He was a realist, yes, and concerned himself with the behavioral truth of acting. His quest, however, was far beyond achieving natural behavior in acting. Stanislavski was an actor, director, and researcher; but the very nature of his search for truth makes him more the spiritual mystic than I or others ever realized. Let us take his enduring question and work as he did to find an answer: What is it that creates artistic inspiration?

E.J. Gold, *And Now for Something Entirely Different,* Pen & Ink,
pencil signed, 11" x 15", Rives BFK,
© 1987 Heidelberg Editions International.

CHAPTER FOUR

THE ANTIDOTE TO NARCISSISM

In today's world, as it was in antiquity, the concept of a spiritual path and the idea of a spiritual person remains culturally bound. Each culture has developed a strong set of expectations and values linked to its own ideas of what "spiritual" means and how it should manifest. A "spiritual person" must fit the role model, the cultural archetype that has been handed down from one generation to the next through oral and/or written traditions. Ceremonies and rituals devised by the houses of worship are in large part formulated to reinforce consensus expectations of the spiritual ideal. For Christians, a spiritual person is expected to have qualities similar to Jesus or the Virgin Mary, in the Middle East a spiritual person must resemble a Rabbi or Muslim Cleric, in the East a spiritual person must wear robes or a loincloth and emulate Buddha or a Hindu priest. Buddhist women in the East are expected to have qualities similar to Kwan Yin, the feminine goddess archetype. Muslim women cover themselves like nomads facing the sandy winds of the desert. Each tribe in Africa or South America has specific modes of behavior and expected dress codes for their shamans and holy men and women. Often, to play the role, you have to look the part.

The point is that we humans view the ineffable, the mystery that animates all life, with lenses that are ground and shaped by the cultural imperatives in which we live. Those imperatives are ingrained, and even if recognized and purposefully rebelled against, they still retain the power to limit our ability to penetrate to the universal; the essential truth that transcends all cultural reference. Being conditioned to experience the world through a cultural lens means that we are, in essence, always playing a role. So, what is the problem with that?

There is nothing inherently negative about cultural conditioning, it is generally harmless and usually quite positive, providing variety and spice to our human experience. It is when cultural context is linked to a fixed sense of personal identity that trouble begins. People who arrange their experiences and relationships in ways that reinforce and buttress their self-image fall into the trap of allowing their search for truth to be yet another device to reinforce their conditioned identity. We can easily become the narcissistic reflection of ourselves; the self-image to which we start to cling, like Narcissus staring at his reflection in the surface of the water.

Luckily, there has been a very powerful, yet very quiet revolution in actor training over the past few decades that introduces a unique approach to this issue. Most importantly, the insights of this revolution can be useful to anyone, not just actors. This approach could have far-reaching benefits for all who experience it and anyone who applies it in his life. It is an approach to acting that honors cultural context and individuality, while generating a direct energy and communion between actors that, ironically enough, could very well be the universal antidote to narcissism.

When a person becomes concerned with the self-image and becomes fixated upon pain and personal history at the expense of communication with others, he is commonly thought to be narcissistic. Actors and performers of all kinds are prone to this pathology due in large part to the extent that their personal vanity is involved in their work. While in some endeavors this tendency can be overlooked, in an actor's work it is deadly.

As we learned from previous chapters, Stanislavski's gift was the formulation of a system of actor training whereby an actor could progress through a series of steps and eventually emerge capable and ready to enact roles on stage or screen with utmost confidence and honesty. As I have discussed earlier, in the first half of the twentieth century members of the Group Theatre in New York City, inspired by Stanislavski's methodologies, began to define a way of acting that led to a cultural renaissance both in the United States and the world at large. Actors, playwrights, film-makers and directors were all inspired by the artistic aspirations of this dedicated group of theatre artists. Soon plays and films were being made to capitalize on the newer, more natural acting associated with the Group Theatre.

One of the group, Lee Strasberg, became famous for his experiments and studio sessions with actors that elaborated upon a certain branch of Stanislavski's work. Mixing elements of Freudian self-analysis and hypnosis, he made it his life's work to help actors mine their interior worlds for emotional veracity. He spent inordinate amounts of time guiding the actor into various states of sensory and emotional recall and then showed how realistic and powerful these states could be when plugged into the circumstances of a text.

While this approach did manage to wean actors from their long-standing penchant for hamming it up and did indeed set in motion a whole new value system that survives today, it also had the unfortunate result of making actors even more self-involved and narcissistic than usual. Another of the group, Stella Adler, also emerged as an influential teacher, although she veered away from Strasberg's approach toward a fuller expression of the imagination and the text.

However, as you may recall, another of the group, Sanford Meisner, chose to concentrate on a particular area of Stanislavski's later work known as the "theory of actions." Meisner recognized that when actors are self-centered, working predominantly from interior, self-generated impulses, they become strangely un-theatrical, strangely over-wrought, and oddly disconnected to the onstage life they so desperately want to enact. On the other hand, when actors manage to bring their attention out of themselves, focusing on the other, they are much more available to stimuli from the outside. When received and acted upon spontaneously, the outside stimuli can establish a basis of rapport that creates very powerful and highly alive performances.

Meisner and those many teachers who employ their own methods of guiding actors into playing actions all help actors to live truthfully within imaginary circumstances. It isn't an easy task. They must be very determined and extremely vigilant early on. It is very difficult to teach this because an actor must by-pass the powerful reflex to conceptualize and intellectually force moments to occur. It takes patience, courage, and the correct mix of intention and trust to allow a truthful flow of emotionally-guided impulses to spark between players.

What follows is a version of what by now are numerous versions of Meisner's basic training mechanism. Keep in mind that only Meisner taught Meisner technique. I am including it here as only one example of the many training exercises developed in recent years. If you or people you know wish to pursue this approach, I recommend seeking out competent and consistent guidance from an acting teacher whose approach to acting comes close to the values herein expressed.

In the beginning, much like someone coming to Zen training for the first time, the actors simply look at the other actor sitting or standing opposite them and they just say what they see. They do not interpret, conceptualize, judge, or in any way distort the information. If I stand opposite someone wearing a white tee shirt, I would simply say, "You're wearing a white tee shirt." The person I am speaking to would simply repeat what she hears: "You're wearing a white tee shirt." I would continue to repeat this observation until there is a natural impulse to change the focus of my attention. I might switch from observing clothing to observing features, and then I might say, "You have brown eyes." My partner would repeat exactly what she has heard, without commentary or distortion. This is necessarily dry, uninteresting, and inexpressive. Too often young actors try to be interesting instead of really talking and listening. In this work, we tell the beginning actor to be *interested* instead of trying to be *interesting*. This level of work is designed to strip away the obligation to entertain while improving the player's focus of attention.

After several passes in this mode with both partners having the chance to be the observer, the exercise would progress to level two. At this next level the observer declares a simple observation just as before except this time the responder repeats in first person. For example, I might say, "You have long hair." And my partner would then reply, "I have long hair."

After several more passes in this level, switching parts, we move on to the next level. This next level begins to incorporate interpretation, and here is where it gets deep. The observer is now allowed to say what she thinks she perceives about the other person's mood, feelings, thoughts, and intentions. Here's what I mean: I might say, "You are confused." My partner has the right now to affirm or deny the interpretation. The partner might respond in question form, "I am confused?" Or a simple denial, "I'm not confused." Or perhaps, "I am confused."

We repeat for some time with this same observation game until I have the genuine impulse to shift my perceptions. The shift might play out like this: "You are confused." "I'm not confused." "You are confused." "I'm not confused." "You are confused." "Yeah, okay, NOW I'm confused!" "You seem irritated." "I seem irritated?" "You seem irritated." "I AM irritated." And so forth. Trust me, it's much more fun to do than to read about. The person making observations has to have the integrity not to make silly or inappropriate statements and the responder has to have the integrity to reply with complete candor.

The more advanced steps include a flowing observer/respondent interaction where the leader switches at random. The stakes go up because the observations begin to be more and more demanding and personal; including observations of when a partner is deflecting, hiding out, avoiding, grandstanding, or bullshitting. These exchanges can become heated, and the pact between serious acting students is that what occurs in the studio is personal artistically, but never "personal" in the ordinary way. They know that by delving and allowing a more honest, non-social self to participate freely in the artistic growth, there will be genuine progress. Without that freedom, no matter how sophisticated the exercise, it will only serve the social mask of the person and the real talent, the hidden treasure of his craft will remain buried.

The core ingredient of all of this work, especially when it moves into the more advanced stages, is that the actor must learn to communicate with a partner in a way that actually inspires him, moves him, and reaches him in an extraordinary way. Playwrights do not write plays about the day nothing happened. The stakes are always high in theatrical texts. Consequently there are numerous scenes where one character is trying hard to change the point of view of the other. Most beginning actors make the mistake of using this attempt to convince the other person through a venting of one's pain or a demonstration of one's feelings or by reporting the problem over and over again with very few variations.

The temptation to report one's pain and to elicit sympathy by the dramatic declaration of one's frustration is typical of a narcissistic approach. It is as if the actor feels that he must portray the audience's point of view of his character or he will not be noticed, he will not fulfill the obvious demands of the text. If one reads the play and surmises that the character is the bad guy, then the actor will usually collaborate with the text and present a character that is rendered as "bad guy."

This way of thinking is understandable. Everyone has a natural tendency to talk about a role from the audience's point of view. However, if an actor plays the role via this perspective, he gets stuck acting general qualities. And in acting, generalities are the enemy to artistic work. Therefore: DO NOT ACT THE AUDIENCE'S POINT OF VIEW! Instead, work diligently to find and act from the genuine point of view of the character. This seems obvious, I know, but it is not as easy as it sounds. It takes lots of practice.

Also remember that from the character's point of view, the attempt to convince, to squelch, to seduce, to inspire, and so forth, virtually all intentions and tactics are always coming from a positive place. That is, an actor must find the "best intention" in each character. Shakespeare's character, Richard III, is a despicable character from the audience's point of view, and although Richard confesses some measure of self-loathing, from his own point of view, he is the soul of wit and charm. To him, his bad behaviors are all necessary to satisfy what he knows will, in the end, be good for everyone—his version of good, his version of making them see the world as he sees it.

Once there is a clear character point of view the actors from that point of view must ask what they are doing. That is, they must not be too fascinated with the problem the character is in, but rather, put the attention on what they are doing to actively get what they really want. To do this they must influence other characters. They must provoke within the other person the courage to fight, the inspiration to start over, the sudden illumination of understanding, and so forth. To accomplish this the actor must get off himself and genuinely reach across and move the heart and soul of the other player.

What fuels this energy is need. The stakes must be high and the actor must use the given circumstances of the play and any personal connections to the situation to engage a true urgency. In other words, this is unlike past methods where an actor would ask, "Why is this happening to me? Why am I saying these things?"—the actor essentially remaining fixated upon the motivation of the character, investing in all the real or imagined events in the character's past that lead them to the present. The modern actor transcends and includes that information and then puts all the attention in each scene upon asking, "What for?" DON'T ASK "WHY?" YOU, AS THE CHARACTER, ARE SAYING

SOMETHING, INSTEAD ASK, "WHAT FOR?" ASK, "I SAY THIS IN ORDER TO *DO* WHAT?"

As I previously said, playwrights do not write plays about the day nothing happened. The characters are all under some kind of pressure and consequently the stakes are always high. To get at what is at stake for a character, the actor must ask, "If I don't get what I want in this scene, what are the consequences?" Her answer must have some heat, it must be important enough to the character to propel her into action.

Modern methods help actors to train the natural reflexes of their instrument so that whatever happens, actors can relax and feel secure that they will remain true and that without their forced intervention, something interesting will emerge. When this happens, each performance is an improvisation, albeit, a highly-structured improvisation with lines and exact staging, but always fresh, always connected to affecting the other.

This new way of working is closer to Jazz improvisation than anything else. The actor knows all the lines, all the notes; however, the rhythms and intonations and subtle under-scorings are entirely dependent upon the fresh rhythms and intonations of the other musicians/actors.

This all sounds fairly straightforward and simple, and, in fact, it is. However, simple does not mean easy. It is not at all easy to go against years of conditioning which nearly always has us dedicated to playing the problem, demonstrating our emotions (acting out), and insisting that the other join our point of view based solely upon the fervor of our insistence.

When this conditioning is dismantled and we begin to assume responsibility for communicating, a fantastic warmth and effortless truth emerges that has all the presence, life-force, danger, nuance, humor, charm, pathos, and thrill one could ever ask for in an actor.

This redirection of energy toward inspiring and truly communing with the other person, truly helping him by fixing his problem, making him see the light, getting the other to move his attention to where you need it to achieve your goal in the scene is paradoxically an act of service. It is generous and selfless, and, ironically enough, when an actor's energy is totally focused on helping the other, great and interesting and uniquely human behaviors pour out. The actor no longer appears as an insecure ego demonstrating its high anxieties onstage, but rather a whole human being engaged in an action. It is quite marvelous to witness.

There is a concept in certain spiritual circles that says one's level of awareness and growth is in a direct ratio to one's level of service. If you are serving only your small self-needs, your level of growth and understanding will match that. If you serve others, your awareness will expand exponentially and your growth will match that. Naturally, if you come to serve groups of people, nations, the globe, the manifest universe, and, of course, God (the Absolute), your growth and understanding will expand in an exponential ratio corresponding to that level of service.

As you can sense, when actors are no longer serving themselves but centered upon serving the other actors and the play as a whole, the potential for growth is amazing. Rather than playing character and returning to the small self, actors under these conditions begin to have character, begin to grow something very fine within themselves that, over time, manifests in a level of humanity well above their self-absorbed counterparts.

The new actor has the chance to grow up. Whereas many actors are drawn to acting because it is an extension of the adolescent need to be special, to make it all about "me" and "my pain," the new actor enjoys the deep confidence and security of knowing that no longer does he need to worship the small egocentric self. The new actor comes to realize that by sacrificing the need to make himself look interesting, he alleviates the suffering of others as well as himself.

In the advanced stages, an actor who has mastered the ability to live truthfully under imaginary circumstances begins to realize what the Buddhists have already known for many centuries: even in ordinary life, circumstances are all imaginary circumstances. When that happens, the actor as a person on the planet resolves personal suffering and comes to realize that he no longer needs to strive to satisfy a self that does not actually exist; at least not in the ordinary way we think of it existing. So, whose suffering gets alleviated? It is a true paradox and a beautiful one to ponder.

E.J. Gold, *Femme au Chapeau Chic avec Popcorn,* Pen & Ink,
pencil signed, 11" x 15", Rives BFK,
© 1987 Heidelberg Editions International.

CHAPTER FIVE

The Tao of Acting

There is a moment in the theatre when something very unique and rare and deeply satisfying happens. The actor and audience merge in a way that defies description. We recognize it when it arrives. Everyone feels it. We know when it "clicks"; when the timing, the breath, the contact is so alive, it transcends ordinary reality and becomes something else, something extraordinary.

That magical moment cannot be forced or manufactured. It manifests indirectly, in a way that is similar to how scientists observe atomic particles in a cloud chamber. They cannot actually see them, but they can observe their effects as they travel through the cloud molecules. In the chamber of the theatre, the effect is sometimes a burst of laughter, a warmth throughout the space, a gasp, or even a stunned silence. These moments hint at something tasted, something deeply experienced outside the tyranny of words.

The ancient Chinese recognized this mystery as a quality inherent in nature. They knew, also, the importance of living in harmony with it. This unnamable quality came to be known as the Tao, which translates as "The Way." As they lived and worked in accordance with it, they recognized that it was a wondrous dynamic consisting of an infinitely complex interplay of "male" and "female" energies. They discovered that the great dance between the female quality (Yin) and the male (Yang) is responsible for all aspects of manifest creation.

Consider a bowl, for example; the outer portion could be said to be Yang since it gives the bowl form and the inner part of the bowl would be Yin since it creates a receptive shape. Indeed, one cannot exist without the other, but the blended interplay of the forms create the function. You can sense Yin and Yang within the structure of the human body quite readily. The inner arm is the Yin while the outer part is the Yang. Touch the outer part of the arm and it feels strong, protected, capable of withstanding force. Touch the inner arm and it feels tender, unprotected, and highly sensitive. Every object, every relationship, every manifest phenomenon can be easily perceived as an interaction between these two energies.

Every word, concept, idea, object, or energy exists in a state that is uniquely dependent upon its opposite for existence. One rather obvious example is light and shadow. One cannot exist without the other. Darkness is only dark in relationship to the concept or existence of light. Less obvious are the ideas of good and evil, wisdom and ignorance, heaven and hell. When one realizes in a deeply personal way that goodness is only good in relationship to bad, one has entered into one of the more sophisticated insights. The notion that something could be all good or that there would emerge a heavenly reality without anything negative is absurd and a false idea to entertain. As Hamlet says to Rosencranz, "… for there is nothing either good or bad, but thinking makes it so."[1]

The Tao, however, is a conceptual framework of a non-dual state whereby opposites are reconciled and integrated. There is no struggle, no resistance, no attempt to force a dominant view since all views exist as a result of the opposite. It is literally a dynamic interwoven unfolding process that when enjoyed with amused awareness brings great happiness and relief from suffering. One bypasses the conflict-driven mind and enters into a new reality that is uniquely unified.

If we take the fundamental principles and apply them to the event of watching a play, we see that in the theatre, the audience is in the dark, sitting in the passive and receptive mode that is Yin. The actors are in the light, in the active mode, which is Yang. The outside of the theatre is Yang and the inside Yin. The empty stage is Yin until the lights go out and the audience becomes Yin and the stage lights come up with the action, transforming it into Yang. Yin is soft, yielding, cool, and feminine. Yang is hard, unyielding, hot, and masculine. Stage movements are an orchestration of the two qualities that guide the focus of the audience and gradually unfold the spectacle.

As the Tao suggests, there is a continuous interplay, a dynamic interdependency of energy that flows. A successful production is one in which there are moments of receptivity as well as moments of active participation on the part of both the audience and players. Live theatre is particularly exciting because each performance has the potential to lift off into a flow dynamic where everyone in the theatre chamber hits a wavelength together. Those moments of collective humanity, akin to what people hope for in a church experience, provide a certain form of sustenance for everyone. At the very least it provides an experience to alleviate the sensation of separation.

From this perspective, good acting is a dynamic flow between players onstage. If an actor is all on output and isn't really listening or responding in the moment, but is instead enacting a replay of a former rehearsal, there is no flow and the performance will lack authenticity. The players will all appear wooden and essentially dead. When, on the other hand, there is a lively give and take of energy, a focused combination of Yin and Yang energy flowing effortlessly between them, the air suddenly becomes electrified with potential, and everyone, including the viewers, is exposed to a level of reality where time and space disappear and the truth, however elusive, is revealed in its subtle and not so subtle form.

The Chinese Yin/Yang symbol of the Tao gives us a clue to the more profound dynamics of the concept. In the Yang side there exists a portion of Yin and in the Yin there is a portion of Yang. And so it is that every actor should have within him a portion of the audience and the audience should have within it a portion of the actor. When this relationship is secured, there is a transcendence, a bonding on a deeper level that awakens the soul and ignites a higher understanding.

Actors have been told time and again, "acting is reacting," "follow your instincts," and the ever popular "play the moment." These are all truisms that try to instill the importance of equilibrium in stagecraft. And as the Taoists know, too much of one quality will cause imbalance and imbalance leads to decay. If an actor is all Yang and obsessively pushy, delivering a performance entirely on output without the Yin quality of listening, the performance will suffer. By the same token, if an actor is too passive, unable to take stage and deliver with heat and drive when necessary, the performance will, of course, fall flat.

All good actors know, if not consciously then unconsciously, how to redistribute their personal composition of energy to suit a particular characterization. A man playing Hamlet, for example, might choose to explore the character's journey from the passive or Yin stage to the active or Yang stage. It might occur gradually over the course of the show as Hamlet begins to see how trapped he is by his excessive Yin qualities. He wrestles with his yielding weaknesses, which are repulsive to him, by lashing out at Gertrude and hiding mentally from Ophelia. Yet, when he finally manages to activate his Yang energy, to take action at long last, it is too unfamiliar, too uncontrolled, too late, and ends in tragedy.

While the interplay between players and audience and between fellow actors onstage is vital, an actor can also apply a similar approach to technical concerns. The Yin and Yang qualities of speech, movement, and breath could all be used to orchestrate the flow of words. This way of viewing acting, as you see, can become increasingly detailed, helping to shape every facet of a performance.

The important thing to remember with this concept of the Tao is not the difference between Yin and Yang, but the dynamic synergy of their relationship. One does not exist without the other; they need each other in order to function. And when all the elements are in order and the equilibrium of energies somehow line up, then there is that magical connection, harmony with the Tao.

There are countless stories of actors who, after a particularly spectacular performance, scratch their heads and marvel at the way everything seemed to flow. They take some credit for being prepared, but most of them bow to the mystery, knowing deep inside that they have been merely part of an event, not the event itself. An echo of this is expressed by Taoist Master Ni Hua Ching:

> Neither does the sage act, it is the power of the Tao that acts through him whether he is overly active or inactive. He simply becomes like a leaf riding the wind of the Tao, unable to tell if he is carrying the wind along or the wind is carrying him. Any individual effort obstructs the flow of this infinite potency.[2]

It would be easy to assume that the path of the Tao is a type of simple-minded "go with the flow" philosophy, but that is not the case. The precepts sound simple, but authentic simplicity is not easy to achieve. The Taoists recognized early that much of man's suffering was due to his own unconscious need for intellectual complexities. This urge to prove himself the most clever creature on earth resulted in an unfortunate habit of unconscious meddling. Certainly today with the advent of world pollution, animal extinction, and nuclear threat, we can see the results of that habit. The Taoist path avoids meddling and instead supports appreciation for what is called *the uncarved block*.[3]

They believe that things in their original simplicity have a natural power and that meddling with that simplicity reduces the power, subjecting it to weaknesses. "Go with your instincts" is a command given to actors to remind them of their own uncarved block, their pure primal power. Too much carving, too much clutter in a role will certainly weaken the power of the performance.

To achieve true simplicity is to be conscious of the dynamic processes in life while participating in harmony with the natural order. One must know when to be active and when to be inactive. Anyone can achieve this level of discernment, but only if he is willing to sacrifice intellectual analysis in favor of awareness. One does not observe in order to quantify or weigh, but to deepen the experience, to enter into it fully with every fiber of one's being in each and every moment. To master this moment-to-moment discernment takes a combination of experience and trust—often referred to as faith.

The ultimate act of faith in the Tao of theatre would be improvisation. It takes a lot of experience to be able to act effectively in an improv and even more to have faith. That is why audiences are so responsive to it. They take great delight in knowing the moment is being constructed *at that precise moment*, for their eyes only! Plus, the actors are forced to play "moment-to-moment" and indeed, when one is acting without a script, acting is definitely "reacting." This is always more exciting, more like a sporting event where the outcome isn't fixed. And when experienced performers, regardless of their milieu, take the improvisational leap of trust, the results can neither be matched nor repeated.

Of course, there isn't a moment that is not happening now. However, actors and audiences often prefer to hide behind the veneer of rehearsed moments (interesting that the word "hearse" lies embedded therein). It clearly seems safer to them that way, but in actual fact, they are in grave danger of letting the performance go dead. Anything not imbued with the vitality of immediacy invites a dull drifting away, a sleepy nodding off. That is not what theatre is all about. All experienced actors know that terrible feeling when the audience begins to drift. During those moments, regardless of the profundity of the project, the actor will feel banal and useless.

That does not mean that rehearsed performances cannot be completely alive. On the contrary, it can become a very enjoyable structured improvisation whereby the structure is the preparation before opening. The best actors know that every moment onstage is an improvisation anyway, no matter the number of shows. The wisest actors come to know that in life, every moment is improvised; there are no second takes.

Essentially then, the Tao of acting is to be simple, present, to act in accord with the natural laws of Yin and Yang, to be spontaneous and true to the moment—while maintaining an energy flow appropriate to the overall equilibrium of the show. When this is accomplished, there is artistry, there is transcendence, there is the Tao of acting.

E.J. Gold, *Ah, How Pleasant It Is to Be Wearing a Hat of Stars,* Pen & Ink,
pencil signed, 11" x 15", Rives BFK,
© 1987 Heidelberg Editions International.

CHAPTER SIX

WHAT IS GOING ON HERE?

Try this sometime: sit in a film or stage audience and during the performance, pull your attention back from the show and ask yourself in a quiet voice, "What is going on here?" As you do this sneak a peek at the faces of the crowd around you. You will be amazed to see them sitting with open faces, enthralled by the artistic event they are witnessing. It might feel like you are a stranger in a strange land, warily observing the inhabitants. Nevertheless, it is remarkably liberating to know that you can choose not to fall into the movie or theatre scene and that sometimes giving attention can occur by pulling it back toward you instead of always getting pulled forward.

It's a fun exercise, if a little strange, but it reveals a function of ordinary consciousness that allows humans to suspend their disbelief and fall into stories being presented. We do it with books, with television and radio, with films, and with stories and performances of all kinds. We are unique in this way. The animal kingdom has its rituals and its patterns, usually associated with mating, but nowhere do we see groups of animals focusing their attention upon other animals that are in the process of pretending to be other animals. It is a uniquely human endeavor, and as such we should take a good look at it.

Now, once the attention has been drawn back and you get a chance to observe the event without being spellbound, you can begin to contemplate movie- or theatre-going with a clearer sense of awareness. Watch how the bodies move, how the faces reflect the mood changes, how the individuals delight in having their attention absorbed into a scene as it unfolds for their pleasure. While observing, ask yourself,

"What is going on here?"

Granted the simplified answer is that it is a form of storytelling and people have always enjoyed storytelling. And yes, there are issues weighed, manners displayed and critiqued, and emotions evoked. But that still does not answer the question. Content aside, what is happening? What is the meaning behind the form? Why go to experience stories? What function is being served?

The standard answers are usually, "Because it is an escape"; "It supplies a necessary communal experience"; "It serves to force people to confront their political or social inertia." True, it does all that. Perhaps not all the time or to the same degree, but yes, it has a very necessary role in social bonding and social discourse.

Those benefits are results, however, and by-products of a process. What is the process? What is going on here?

Allow me to provide some food for thought. In order to do this properly, I'm going to have to borrow, albeit lightly, from the world of physics. I hope to do this with clarity and simplicity, and there is no one better suited to help illuminate my point than inventor and biomedical engineer, Itzak Bentov. Bentov is the author of two outstanding books on quantum mechanics, books that exquisitely describe in layman's terms what has revolutionized physics and all related fields.

Currently, scientists realize that all matter, at the subatomic level, is really a pattern of energy that moves and reacts according to very unpredictable laws. Astonishingly, this energy shows up as waves as well as particles, a fact that still mystifies the scientific community. These energies interact with other energies, and that interaction results in the various phenomena we call matter.

Sound is a wave energy emitted from a resonating system. Our heart, Bentov is quick to point out, is also a resonating system. The brain gives off waves as do our bodies. In actuality, we as humans participate in a miraculous, electromagnetic and thermodynamic energy wave event on this planet. We are not just clumps of inert pulsing hydrogen and carbon-based material. We are conscious vibratory energy that takes in and emits and participates in the whole fantastic light show.[1]

It is worth considering that sometimes this resonating, vibratory creature we call a human being gets curious enough to want to learn about its fundamental construct, its vibratory energy. Could anyone need more proof that the universe is alive and conscious? The universe is clearly conscious since we as a species are clearly an expression of the universe and we have the ability not only to be aware, but to be aware of our awareness. In addition, and most uniquely our gift and curse, we have the ability to represent our findings to ourselves in various symbolic forms. In order to do that, however, we create the illusion that we are somehow distinct from that stuff out there with which we interact.

Interestingly enough, when energy waves interact and if they are too different, they will assume a beat frequency, creating periodic moments where they cancel each other out. Sometimes, however, they can reach a kind of understanding and *rhythm entrainment* occurs. This means they give up their little differences in favor of a new frequency. This new frequency has the potential to be a coherent wave pattern—that means little or no modulation in the pattern—in other words, unified.[2]

Another aspect of vibration is the fact that if a certain frequency is activated, say, a note on a piano, other frequencies will respond in sympathy. Pluck middle C and the C strings of other octaves will vibrate, as will certain other notes in mathematical sympathy to the original.[3]

Consider the audience as a massive oscillating system, a veritable battery of energy. When they are led to focus their energy upon a single character or event, the performer in the primary spotlight will receive a dose of energy outside the normal experience. If the performer has had training and preparation, she can charge her instrument with the additional energy and, through skillful means, transform it into a strong and effective impression. She can strike a chord within herself, and the soul of the audience will often respond in sympathetic vibration.

If the performer's instrument is damaged or unable to handle the sudden jolt of energy, she will usually close off her own energy, deflect with a shielding, or sometimes allow the energy to distort the performance. This lack of preparation is sensed by the audience, of course, and governs their willingness to focus their complete attention. If you lose the attention of the audience, the show becomes dull and ineffective and, well, fails. The quality of performance, then, in the purest sense, is really a vibratory event.

The battery of energy provided by an audience depends upon a number of factors, not the least of which is expectation. Every audience comes into the theatre with a layer of expectation, and that energy is what the performer encounters first. When a comedian is successful and generally accepted as funny, the energy of the audience's expectation provides a free ride. He or she must still fulfill the expectation, but the atmosphere is initially charged in the comedian's favor. A less known performer faces a low expectation energy and must work to overcome it.

Using Bentov's vibratory model, during the course of a performance that is clicking, the variety of wave formations in the house and onstage have ceased the occasional canceling (beat frequency) and everyone can enjoy frequent and sustained moments of rhythm entrainment. You've no doubt seen birds flying in remarkable synchronicity; that is another example of rhythm entrainment. During a good performance, the actors and the audience are, in a way, flying together.

The experience of theatre then, could be said to be simply for the pleasure of flying. I believe, however, that the pleasure, and even flying, is a by-product of a process even more subtle and necessary.

The Russian mystic and teacher, G.I. Gurdjieff, introduced to his group of students a system of study that, among other things, outlines man's position in the hierarchy of cosmic energy. His system, although new to Western man, had been in use many years in the Near Eastern mystery schools. It was a version of the table of elements, based upon what was called, "the law of the octave," in other words waves, vibrations.

According to this system, as interpreted by P.D. Ouspensky, man's potential and sole hope of advancement is dependent upon the collection and proper absorption of substances Gurdjieff called "hydrogens." In this system, the basic substances for maintaining life are hydrogens H768, H192, and H384; food, air, and water. What was surprising to many of his students was also the inclusion of hydrogens 48, 24, and 12—representing impressions as a major source of life-sustaining substance. In fact, Gurdjieff explained that impressions were the *most important* substance.[4]

If we consider carefully the implications of this, we can begin to see why people go to the theatre, or to the movies, or to museums, and so on. They are literally being fed. Of course their ability to digest the impressions they encounter is a different matter and a constant frustration to artists everywhere.

We have all experienced a taste of what Gurdjieff was talking about. Exposure to a magnificent meteor shower, an original Van Gogh painting, or a masterpiece film can energize and lift the spirits.

If we accept this model, what we see going on in the theatre is this: a group of individual energy fields collect themselves into a contained space, and through the help of some careful manipulation of mood, they relinquish the focus of their individual energy fields onto the stage. Then, other humans who have been trained to handle it, take on an additional charge, transmuting it into refined impressions which serve as food for the audience. Ideally, it is good food that raises their vibratory level.

If their job is done well, the actors are rewarded with an accelerated vibrational wash (applause), plus the expanded consciousness their art affords them. Not to mention the satisfaction of knowing their work may be serving to upgrade the vibratory level of a set of fellow oscillators, improving the entire field for everyone.

This concept is a far cry from the image of a bunch of coarse actor misfits who want to parade their personalities in blatant self-promotion. Of course, it is an impractical perspective for unskilled performers who have not reached a level of objective awareness. Even for the advanced actor, this is only a hint at the possible true function of theatre.

To get to the real heart of the matter, one has to be willing to ask more questions, not to settle for the answer that seems like a complete answer. One could say an audience goes to the theatre to be fed in the form of impressions, and be satisfied with the answer. It sounds pretty good.

However, one should never be satisfied. Let's delve deeper. Being fed? Why? For what purpose? And if they receive this "food," do they also give it? What is the nature of this food? If it's true that you are what you eat, does that apply to impressions as well? I challenge you to continue to ask: What is going on here?

E.J. Gold, *Pierrot de la Lune,* Pen & Ink,
pencil signed, 11" x 15", Rives BFK,
© 1987 Heidelberg Editions International.

CHAPTER SEVEN

THE CHALLENGE OF AWAKENING

Thanks to a number of scientific studies, we are beginning to be able to more openly discuss and explore the various states and stages of human consciousness. Although there are certainly subcategories, the three basic states that most people agree upon are waking, sleeping, and deep dreamless sleep. Waking states refer to our ordinary outer-world condition; our day-to-day existence. Sleeping refers to our nocturnal rest state where, like most organic life on the planet, we place ourselves out of harm's way, usually at night, and sleep. During that rest period, we enter into a vast universe, a subtle, luminous, and intimate realm of dreams. There we have many experiences that occur without the usual constraints and boundaries associated with our ordinary waking state. In addition, at some time during the night, we transition into another state, a deep dreamless state where we exist in a kind of formless, unbounded stillness.

Naturally there are other distinctions of consciousness. Trauma, for instance, will often induce shock; blood sugar imbalances might bring on states of euphoria or depression; certain forms of stress may result in extraordinary feats of strength, endurance, or mental acuity. Many can relate to the "automatic pilot" state, where suddenly you realize you are home and you don't really recall the drive. Those and other familiar states, even the heightened ones, that we take to be part and parcel of our awake consciousness, are considered to be "sleep" states by the great teachers.

If these states that, by all accounts, are considered the normal part of human experience can be considered to be sleep states, then what is the nature of the awakened state? What is this special state of awakened consciousness described by enlightened sages for eons and where does it fit into the scheme of things? More importantly, how can this state be accessed and for what aim?

It is not surprising that the starting premise for nearly all spiritual paths is the recognition that you are asleep; not just spacing out or day-dreaming now and then; you are asleep. Just because you walk and talk and even manage to impress others with your witty remarks, according to the great spiritual traditions, you are not necessarily awake. This is perhaps the hardest hurdle of all since most of us are so enamored of our functional abilities, we have great difficulty accepting this premise. That is why many early exercises in mystery schools serve purely the function of exposing the sleep state. It is the first premise, and when fully experienced, it is the first shock that seekers must endure if they are to make any progress at all.

From what I have experienced, the classic formula for awakening is a *profound recognition of the sleep state* followed by *expert prepa-ration and guidance* toward awakening. In most cases, the awakened state is not entirely foreign to the seeker who wishes to awaken. Glimpses of it have occurred in early childhood, or during a traumatic event, or in moments of deep contemplation, and often it has alerted the person to a new possibility. From all accounts, when fully realized, it is a state that defies verbal description but is generally thought of as a timeless, fearless state of unity and bliss, mixed with a strong intuitive understanding of the cosmic mysteries.

What's more, the understanding of the cosmic mysteries usually manifests in the form most suited to the individual. That is, a compos-er might suddenly understand the laws of creation through music, a poet through poetry, a gardener through gardening, and so on. That is why it is important for people to follow their natural talents, for it is within the framework of their work that the awakening will unfold and the knowledge will be given.

It is difficult to imagine entering into a state of being that you either have not recognized as awake or that you have been conditioned away from or even locked out of by the overwhelming power of the marketplace world. I was at a Sufi workshop once when a young woman, newly arrived for the day's work, remarked to the teacher that being in the space made her feel as if she were being hypnotized. His answer was sublime and clearly outlined for me the dilemma facing anyone entering into spiritual work. He said, "What makes you think you aren't already hypnotized?"

There it was: the age old struggle between what we hold on to as our idea of reality and the risk, the leap of faith one must make in order to examine it and to explore beyond it in a very serious search for what is really real. In relation to this, I find it useful to return to the basics and to science, modern man's avowed arbiter of what is real. What science has proved is that our brains function at different wavelengths depending upon the states we are experiencing and, interestingly enough, we experience different states depending upon the wavelengths themselves.

We create a combination of brain waves in our daily lives; however, the dominant wave pattern our brains produce is called a beta frequency. Beta waves are considered to be between 13 and 100 cycles per second. The higher frequencies, those that are 35 hertz (cycles per second) or more, are associated with anxiety, distress, and even panic. However, in the lower range we can associate it with alertness, concentration, and focus. When we are fully engaged in a task, however, focusing in a mindful way or absorbed in a good book, or in any way allowing ourselves to commit to the full sensual experience of attention, we enter into the alpha state, 8-12.9 hz, where we experience more ease, more clarity, and a reduction of mental stress. When, under specific circumstances the brainwaves enter into even deeper states, usually associated with meditation or during REM and dream-filled sleep, our brains activate the theta wave patterns, 4-7.9 hz. In these states one enters into another reality, and if active while conscious, one may experience hallucinations of such visceral force as to appear real. While this dreamlike stage may resemble madness, it is simply the strange theta wave wonderland that exists just before reaching the ultimate brain wave pattern called "delta."[1]

In delta wave patterns, the person is considered to be in the deep dreamless sleep state. This is a super Samadhi state, absent of all qualities including the quality of absence. It is what the Hindus might call "pure consciousness." We enter into this state every night, and because it has no objects, no patterns or textures, it lies outside our ordinary consciousness. The dream state where the subtle realm is active has many references to our daily lives, surreal and absurd ones to be sure, but clearly utilizing the colors, structures, and often the characters from our lives. This state can be recalled from memory and verified as an experience and is, therefore, widely known and widely studied.

Less known, however, is the deep dreamless delta wave state. Less known because upon entering this level of consciousness most people black out. They may have experienced deep delta waves and landed directly where the profound structures of all of creation and the ultimate answers reside; what Carl Jung called the "collective unconscious," but they just don't remember it. It is interesting to note that during deep meditation, the delta state can be accessed in a particular way that is not wholly unconscious as long as small amounts of the other brain waves accompany the state. For those whose awareness has consciously entered into the state, it is profoundly life altering, yet enormously difficult to describe. What they all report, however, is that the experience is a non-dual experience, meaning it has no opposite to give it contrast and comparison. A great feeling of expansive one-ness is experienced during the delta state, but words cannot do it justice since they are necessarily bound to a dualistic framework. Therefore, the essential quality of the experience can only be hinted at through reference and suggestion, like describing a flavor.

I can explain the recipe for an apple pie, for example, and I can describe the visual experience, the smell, and the texture of the freshly baked pie, and I can even describe the delicious taste, but the taste, the actual experience of it requires, more than words can ever supply. At some point, you will have to take a bite and actually taste it yourself.

What has been reported from those who have tasted pure consciousness is that when immersed in the state, the individual is exposed to the timeless, boundless universal Self, that area of awareness that unites us all. It is at this pure stage of transcendent bliss, this "pure awakening," that individuals taste the one universal taste, and in a flash, they know, really know, that they have nothing more to fear. Death is not the end any more than birth is the beginning. It is through the taste of this that the ordinary, fearfully shielded and trapped mind is finally liberated. One finally learns who one is, and when that is known, it is easier to know what to do and how to do it. One is finally awake.

For all seekers on the path toward awakening, a guide is needed to help discern between real awakenings and false, imaginary ones. These guides can pace a student's growth to help him or her to arrive at their highest potential. The methods employed by the guides are many, and each student requires slightly different treatment to insure safe and effective passage through the labyrinth.

Vital to a successful methodology of training in this area is a clear understanding of the difference between "states" and "stages." A teacher can provide the circumstances and the keys to delve into and experience levels of consciousness. However, a truly competent teacher does not allow the student to become enamored of "states" of consciousness. What really matters is enough repeated experience with the states until they become permanent acquisitions. An accomplished guide can help students sustain their progression of awareness until it becomes fully established in their natural and organic expression. Their awareness expands to include all brain wave states, readily accessed at any time.

There are, however, some basic recurring formats. For example, nearly all teachers start with some form of relaxation and a device to focus the attention. Some concentrate on the breath, others on doing tasks slowly, others rely on massage or visualization journeys. These are all techniques geared toward establishing a ground of readiness wherein new levels of consciousness are introduced.

Actors, like everyone else, must deal with stress, sometimes with an inordinate amount, so they, too, know, perhaps now more than ever, the importance of managing their stress so that it will not impede the flow of creative energy.

The challenge facing actors with a desire to awaken spiritually is that the spiritual quest actually induces stress—not the stress normally associated with pressure in the work-a-day world—but stress nonetheless. It catapults the seeker into a labyrinth of study, self-evaluation, rigorous demands, and relentless dedication. Therefore, those actors who are also wanting to awaken in this life must undergo a journey of preparation that is a very specialized mix of relaxation and spiritual stress factors that are sometimes administered in the form of expertly timed conscious shocks.

These shocks, once the natural by-product of living in a primitive environment, must now, due to contemporary buffers, be administered through participation in spiritual work.[2] Some shocks are provided at first by the teacher, but are eventually the responsibility of the student. The shock might come in the form of a Zen master's blasting shout, a sudden and unexpected admonition, a public invitation to sing, an unexplained wave of warmth and love, or in countless other forms, depending upon the creativity and temperament of the teacher.

These shocks are used to boost the vibratory frequency of the student at properly timed intervals so as to facilitate new understanding. The knowledge of when and how much of a shock to administer is a very delicate science and must be given to the student by only the most qualified of teachers.

What is happening is that through the actions of the teacher, the student's brain waves are forced to deal with an overload. This momentary chaos and stress upon the system forces the brain to restructure neural networks in order to handle the new stress.[3] Constructive shocks of this nature, if they are to be of any value, must occur through what some teachers call the "law of necessity." Only a truly awakened and expert teacher responds fully to this law and knows when and where and how to administer these shocks.

The law of necessity follows the precept that the cosmos is alive and opens to the energy generated by the pure intention associated with real need and is only faintly responsive to simple desires. An extreme example from life is the story of the woman whose child was accidentally struck and trapped by a car. In an instant, and gathering energy resources well outside the norm, she lifted the car and freed her child. This, of course, is a feat normally impossible for a human being, yet the law of necessity made it possible for her to access powerful, apparently miraculous energy.

In similar fashion, by placing the element of necessity into a task, the actor/adept can perform amazing feats. Grotowski, the famed Polish theatre researcher and director, made use of this fact when in his early experiments he would ask his actors to do extraordinary and hugely demanding physical exercises. In one he would ask his actors to dive roll over fellow actors who were lying on their backs, shoulder to shoulder on the gym mat. The number of actors on the mat gradually increased, forcing the actors to dive farther and farther in order to avoid landing on one of their compatriots. This exercise yielded remarkable feats of physical ability and gave the actors enormous courage and confidence.

The added dimension of necessity creates, as you can imagine, a very real element of stress, albeit a constructive variety of stress. A friend of mine, studying with an influential teacher, told of how he and others were taken for many miles to a special work session at a casino. There they were practicing their various levels of attention when the teacher gave word that each student had to get back to the school using only his/her winnings. Unfortunately, by the time my friend got the news, he had lost nearly all his money.

Not wanting to be left there in the city, my friend became intensely focused, knowing he would rather not have to hitchhike back to the school. As a result, he put all of his attention to work with the last few dollars he owned. His awareness boosted to a new level, he began following a different set of impulses, and soon, much to his surprise and relief, he started to win. He played until he made ample travel fare and then quit while he was ahead.

These examples demonstrate that it is possible consciously and successfully to springboard off of constructive stress into new territories of awareness and accomplishment. For actors, an audience can provide just such a springboard. The expectant energy of an audience is a form of necessity that most seasoned actors grow to enjoy. The stress of performance lifts them above themselves and charges their work with a palpable wakefulness. During rehearsals, a good director, like a good spiritual taskmaster, provides similar conditions of necessity and stress in order to liberate the finest from the actors. From what I see, it is this boost of awareness that first hooks people into working in the theatre. The show must go on, the timing and energy must crest in specific waves, and the actors awaken to the vivid virtual reality before them in an intoxicating rush of ensemble cooperation and personal endeavor.

Mystery schools and brotherhoods working to awaken from the sleep state often work in groups in very similar ways; using the group energy to activate a field of energy similar to that of a theatrical cast before an audience. Sometimes they meditate for long periods of time, achieving stress through enforced periods of concentration, encounters with nothingness or mortality. Sometimes they meet face to face with the master teacher and must supply a response to a question or koan they have been pondering for months. The list goes on and on, there are countless constructive stress factors used in the spiritual training business.

One important, but little known stress factor used in some mystery schools, and one that actors could also effectively use, is the tolerance of negative manifestations of others. That is to say, simply being in the presence of others who are sources of irritation for you or who provide stressful negative energy could actually work to awaken you. The key word in the technique is, tolerate. You must not be drawn into the negativity, but remain attentive, sensing the effect it has on your organism.

Regarding this, St. Abba Dorotheus, one of the early Desert Fathers from the Benedictine Trappist order, says this:

> Over whatever you have to do, even if it be very urgent and demands great care, I would not have you argue or be agitated. For rest assured, everything you do, be it great or small, is but one eighth of the problem, whereas to keep one's state undisturbed even if thereby one should fail to accomplish the task, is the other seven-eighths …. If, however, in order to accomplish your task you would inevitably be carried away and harm yourself or another by arguing with him, you should not lose seven for the sake of preserving one eighth.[4]

And really, this is parallel to the teaching of Jesus, who asks his followers to "turn the other cheek." However, it takes training and much practice to turn the other cheek. And that is another reason why there is emphasis on groups, schools, and monastic orders. Ideally, within those controlled environments, a person can test his ability to turn his cheek on a regular basis until it becomes deeply ingrained and authentic.

I am reminded of a story about Roy Hart, a promising young actor studying at the Royal Academy in London years ago. He went to study voice with a teacher named Alfred Wolfsohn, who had a reputation as a particularly gifted teacher. At the first lesson, Roy told Alfred that he was frustrated in acting class because he was working on playing Othello, but could not connect at all with the character, because Othello murders Desdemona, and Roy knew he himself was not a murderer and didn't seem to have it in him.

Alfred listened and simply moved on to their lesson. As the lesson progressed, he began to insult and berate Roy at every turn. They soon began to argue, whereupon Alfred only re-doubled his provocations until, finally, an enraged Roy erupted in a violent outburst declaring that he wanted to kill Alfred. At that moment, Alfred dropped his attack, smiled, and said, "So, now we see the murderer. It is best to find him in your art, lest he sneak out unexpectedly in life." Roy went on to study extensively with Mr. Wolfsohn, later developing his own work in the form of a theatre company—The Roy Hart Theatre.

The point is this: mastering our flaws at the deepest level takes artistry and technique that must be developed over time through the continued exposure to irritants and the equally continuous exercise of tolerance.

For years I thought this was a relatively new technique, used only in the West, until I came across the following quote in the *Annals of the Hall of Blissful Development* by Huang Yuan-chi, a Chinese adept who lived during the Yuan dynasty. He states:

> People are happy when there is quiet and vexed when there is commotion. Don't they realize that since their energy has already been stirred by the clamor of people's voices and the involvements and disturbances of people and affairs, rather than use this power to be annoyed at the commotion, it is better to use this power to cultivate stability. An ancient said, "When people are in the midst of the disturbance, this is a good time to apply effort to keep independent." Stay comprehensively alert in the immediate present, and suddenly an awakening will open up an experience in the midst of it all that is millions of times better than quiet sitting. Whenever you encounter people making a commotion, whether it concerns you or not, use it to polish and strengthen yourself, like gold being refined over and over again, until it no longer changes color. If you gain power in this, it is much better than long drawn out practice in quiet.

I hope you can see the significance of this concept. It not only shatters the myth of needing to retreat to a cave somewhere to meditate alone in quiet, but it implies that staying calm amid the clamor of life, practicing an emotional Tai Chi, is a million times more beneficial! And where better than the theatre to find such clamor!

Also, it is important to note that with all this recent cultural insistence upon relaxation, one should remember that it is a good thing only if used to counteract the wrong kinds of stress. If not, it is useless and, indeed, counterproductive if it diminishes the possibility for constructive stress and full engagement with life. Viva the tumult if it can train the soul!

It should be evident by now that the actor's world is ideally suited for the process of awakening. The inherent constructive stress factors continue to refine the nervous system, to expose the actor to a wide variety of brain wave states that certainly shift to alpha, theta, and possibly delta. Unfortunately, the problem at present, in my estimation, is that Western theatre, unlike the craft in Asia, enjoys no culturally-acceptable tradition of spiritual progress.

In the Eastern theatre, the traditional theatrical forms maintain their contact with religious celebrations, shamanistic rain dances, contemplative wisdom, meditation practices, fertility rites, and other rituals. They are in a mystic partnership with the forces of the universe. While it is true that many Asian countries retain theatrical traditions that value and encourage spiritual progress, those traditions have recently shown signs of erosion.

In today's world, both East and West endure a rapid acceleration of materialism and an increasing level of fragmented spiritual disciplines. The world is, in fact, fast becoming a huge, swarming marketplace, a marketplace within which actors must continue to work.

To the spiritually inclined, the marketplace seems to be the enemy, a distraction pulling them from their highest aims. Not so for the artist who knows not only the value of transmuting the clamor, but the elements of this art that are integral to spiritual awakening.

In acting, for example, training in the tolerance of others can begin immediately, with no special instruction. By working for the good of the show, and by tolerating the negative manifestations of others—or even of oneself—one is developing the internal power necessary to do the same in life.

Consider that in nearly every cast there will be personality types that rub other personality types the wrong way, that inspire intolerance, or worse. Yet, the irritation of personality clashes must ultimately be endured for the sake of the show. This does not imply total impunity for disruptive or dangerous behavior; people who behave that way must be expelled for the good of the whole. Yet, refinement of the nervous system occurs through the very real internal work of cooperating together to make the show succeed, regardless the inevitable frictions. Under these conditions, any negative feelings that erupt are all fuel for progress. They are actually instrumental in establishing real presence, a necessary step toward awakening.[5]

But what is the purpose of the awakened state? Why attempt such a change in consciousness at all? Well, that's just it. Most people are content to carry on under the illusion that they are the masters of their lives. They live their lives in semi-darkness and in perpetual existential anguish. They view their quiet suffering as "reality" and think nothing more of it. They try to fill the emptiness with myriad compulsions and sensory stimulation, to no avail. And it is the great vanity of most people that keeps them in darkness, convinced they are already awake.

When, however, due to an unusual shock, an accidental awakening occurs. and the person gets a glimpse of real human possibility, he or she becomes forever hounded by that newly-seen potential.

If one can manage to pull away from the rush of daily sensation and cultural demands long enough to begin self-cultivation, the advantages of awakening become increasingly evident.

There is, however, a slight glitch in the process. It's not all peaches and cream. The automatic part of us, the machine you might say, wants peaches and cream and wants to keep its dominant position as the pleasure-seeking ruler of the house. Obviously, there is an inner conflict that has to be dealt with intelligently.

One way is to be aware of the defense mechanisms existing in the organism, sometimes referred to as the machine, because it is composed primarily of compulsions and conditioning in the form of automatic habits. Regarding this, E.J. Gold, high-tech shaman, transformational psychologist, and author of *The Human Biological Machine As A Transformational Apparatus*, says the following:

> The initial discomfort during the process of entering the waking state from the sleeping state is the principal reason we fall back into the sleeping state. ... When the machine first comes to life, we may find the experience too excruciating, too emotionally, mentally, and physically painful, too exhausting, and we may decide to allow the machine to fall back into sleep.
>
> Eventually if the machine remains in the sleeping state, gangrene will set in and the machine will die. This is the chief cause of ordinary death. If the machine were awake, it would also eventually die, but not in the same way. [6]

So you see, there is ample warning that the path toward awakening may not be entirely pleasant. Yet, anyone who is called to awaken knows deep inside the value of enduring momentary discomfort for the chance to evolve and serve all sentient beings.

In summary, there are a number of things in the theatre which can lend themselves to spiritual refinement and the awakened state, namely: developing the actor's instrument to orchestrate his four bodies (moving, emotional, intellectual, and instinctual); creating inner strength by tolerating the negative manifestations of others; enacting archetypes and entities from the collective unconscious; and, if the actor is fully awake, consciously journeying to universal realms, giving his work a range and power equaling the master painters, composers, and thinkers of all time. To do this, however, the actor must develop that which can operate and exist in those realms. That is the subject of my next chapter.

E.J. Gold, *Harlequin of Lesser Birds,* Pen & Ink,
pencil signed, 11" x 15", Rives BFK,
© 1987 Heidelberg Editions International.

CHAPTER EIGHT

HIGHER BODIES

A truly masterful actor who enters into the creative state during performance utilizes every part of his being in order to expand his antennae of awareness and to live fully within two worlds at once. He is living through a very comprehensive adventure whereby the various levels of his gross and subtle body are working in a unified way to maintain the blended realities. He is spontaneously experiencing foreground and background, text and context, inner life and outer expression, time and timelessness. He is, in effect, activating his higher bodies in a way that serves the text and vivifies each moment on stage.

The notion of "higher bodies" seems far-fetched to some because they most likely conjure images borrowed from bad movies. However, if you take an honest appraisal of what the term "higher bodies" really means, the idea no longer seems so outlandish. To begin, let's consider that we already have a series of very recognizable "bodies" in the form of discrete biological systems. We have a skeletal system, a muscle system, a nervous system, a cardiovascular system, a lymphatic system, a digestive system, and so forth. Each of these systems operates independently within its own unique set of rules while being fully integrated into the whole organism.

It is naïve to think that our human systems are limited only to those lower ones we have so far catalogued and can see with our eyes. There are higher energy systems, long recognized by metaphysics that are only recently being recognized by science. Anyone who has experienced acupuncture, for example, can attest to its effectiveness, yet, acupuncture is a medical practice that depends entirely upon a network of invisible energy lines. There are, in fact, increasing numbers of fully- accepted and commercially available items of modern convenience that rely upon invisible forces. Very few people have ever seen an actual microwave, for example. It is only our fixation on outdated images of our bodies that keeps us in ignorance about our true nature.

Itzak Bentov, in his book, *Stalking the Wild Pendulum*, states that our physical bodies, which are in essence, on the micro-foundational level, interacting energy wave patterns, will inevitably, like all interactive wave patterns, contain higher harmonics (You may recall the example of striking middle C on the piano causing a sympathetic vibration with the other Cs).[1]

He contends that there do exist other "bodies" made up of higher harmonics of our physical body. They, of course, may not look like our physical body, but they exist, vibrating like other piano strings at relative frequencies. Our emotional body is one harmonic, the mental another, the subtle another, the psychic another, and so forth.

Bentov further contends that we are, in a way, a radio-like device, receiving four or five different "stations" simultaneously. Under ordinary circumstances we are unable to hear the subtle non-physical stations, because the physical station is usually blaring so loudly. If we manage to quiet the loud physical stations, we can tune in to the higher harmonics and come to know ourselves more fully.

An actor who has committed to an action, who has established rich and complex character relationships onstage, who has prepared the emotional terrain, and whose instrument is in full support of the imaginary circumstances can actually succeed in silencing the usual internal voices of dissent and confusion. He enters into a rarified space where time and space are elastic and each breath has meaning. The loud stations are quiet and the quiet ones can now be heard.

By tuning in to the higher frequencies, we align our instrument with higher and higher realities. Eventually, and often after great struggle and sacrifice, we have the possibility to voluntarily access higher states of awareness that correspond to what is often described as other realms. For the actor, the realms are transcendent shared realities suffused with the heat and passion of onstage life urgency.

The awareness and experience of higher harmonics in order to investigate and relate to other dimensions is the alchemical impetus behind most religions, although most keep this idea hidden. As we might expect, there are differing opinions as to the names and qualities of the bodies and realms. The differences in rendering are usually a matter of cultural inclinations, reflecting the tastes and habits of local customs and legends. Nevertheless, they refer to the same universal states and stages associated with our human journey.

The ancient as well as modern Taoists concern themselves almost exclusively with the cultivation of higher bodies—particularly the crystal body, which is sometimes called the diamond body. These bodies, if correctly cultivated, will result in a balanced and righteous life on earth and a conscious immortality. That is to say, instead of death sweeping the soul into the cycle of reincarnation, the integrity of the complete crystal body passes on to a heavenly realm of its own actualization.[2]

For the Taoist, the initial and primary method of cultivation is the collection and proper distribution of chi (or Prana in the Indian system). Chi is the elemental and invisible life force energy that circulates along pathways called meridians. Once the meridians of the body have been cleared and cleansed, the chi can begin to collect in preparation to awaken the higher harmonics. In relation to this, here is what Gurdjieff, as reported by Ouspensky, says:

> If the physical organism begins to produce a sufficient quantity of these fine substances [hydrogens], and the "astral body"within it becomes formed, this astral organism will require for its maintenance less of these substances than it needed during its growth. The surplus from these substances can then be used for the formation and growth of the "mental body" which will grow with the help of the same substances that feed the "astral body," but of course the growth of the "mental body" will require more of these substances than the growth and feeding of the "astral body." The surplus ... will go to the growth of the fourth body.[3]

The ever popular *out-of-body* experience relates to the ability of the astral form to detach from the body and consciously travel. We, of course, do this every night in our sleep. But to be conscious of the process and actually to experience this plane of reality in a lucid form, well, that's something else entirely. Some actors report experiences of heightened awareness where they indeed experienced an out-of-body experience. They seemed to be both onstage and in the audience simultaneously, unified as seer and seen.

There are countless cases cited of this phenomenon, yet science, when it deigns to address the issue, remains unable or unwilling to take a stand. Nevertheless, there is mounting evidence that the human instrument is indeed capable of such a state.

Brian Bates, a psychologist who spent seven years researching the psychology of acting with students at the Royal Academy of Dramatic Art in London, has done experiments in which he helped guide an actor's consciousness to detach itself and roam around the building, reporting continuously along the way. Although the observations of the traveling actor were uncanny in their detail, and even though the actor afterwards was convinced he had left his body and traveled about the building, Bates still injects a kind of skepticism, implying it might be a hypnotic fantasy, born out of the power of an actor's imagination.[4]

But what is imagination? It strikes me as a form of laziness to think that because we have a name for some function of our being, we can assume we understand it. The imagination might be operating under a certain set of laws yet undiscovered. Yet, because it is ignored, it has been relegated to the fancies of children and is, therefore, absent from any serious scientific inquiry.

Consider that light is not really visible until we receive it in the retina—which is a limited, although wonderful sensor. And we humans are privy to only a certain spectrum of light waves in a vast world of waves. And, astonishingly, we see only those light rays that have been rejected from the electromagnetic masses we perceive as "objects." In that way, if you want to get right down to it, when we are operating in the daily manifest realm, we are actually living in the rejected universe. We see what didn't make it through the object and that creates the visual display of these energy fields. If we rub our eyes we can witness an array of kaleidoscopic effects. What of that? Is it just nerves creating images? How? Why the patterns?

And from where comes the illumination in our dreams? Is this not light? Perhaps it is the memory of light. Even if it is memory, it is perceived as light. And isn't it mind-boggling that a function in the brain can reproduce light, an energy traveling at roughly 186,000 miles per second? From where does that kind of mental energy originate?

Most stunning of all is to consider the famed Penfield and Perot experiments where two top Toronto brain surgeons touched various parts of their patient's brain with low level electrodes while the patients remained awake to report their experience. They discovered that the induced stress in discrete parts of the brain would manifest for the patient full blown memory replays as well as hallucinations. The patients saw and heard, smelled and sensed, and even experienced emotions stimulated and triggered by the placement of the electric stimulation.[5] What was never recognized in that data and something that is so obvious as to be elusive is the fact that never once did they find the home of the "observer." Yes, there were all these effects induced by electric stimulation, but where does the observer reside, the experiencer, the one having the hallucination and reporting on it?

I bring this up because I think settling for "it's only imagination" is avoiding the most important part of the equation. The actor/shaman has the ability to develop contact with the deepest, most mysterious parts of the human soul. Having the powers of imagination and concentration that actors have is obviously a pre-requisite for expanded consciousness and experiences well beyond the consensus ordinary reality. The non-ordinary states of awareness bring great insight and comfort to those voyagers who have had the experience. Many actors and performers of all kinds report the mysterious and deeply rewarding effects associated with transcending the ordinary and entering into powerful expanded states.

Having such powers, however, does not imply having success; success meaning *having created that which lasts beyond the veil.* As philosopher and educator Ken Wilber has articulated, the work is to move from temporary states to permanent traits.[6] Having the tools does not mean that one has the plan. One must have both. And to work properly, avoiding mistakes that could be very serious, one needs a guide. One needs expert coaching in these matters and above all, an honest aim. Formulating a true aim outside the usual curiosity-seeking mentality in concert with expert guidance will protect the voyager from harm and insure real progress, measurable and irrefutable progress, capable of withstanding the test of timelessness and the unbearable lightness of being.

E.J. Gold, *The Stars Are My Thoughts,* Pen & Ink,
pencil signed, 11" x 15", Rives BFK,
© 1987 Heidelberg Editions International.

CHAPTER NINE

Higher Purpose

Most of the recent teachings getting popular exposure lately, by healers, psychologists, and a few religious leaders, have one recurring directive in common: they all ask you to love yourself. Loving yourself, they say, will begin to heal blocks and bring you gently into a more powerful, balanced state of being.

While noble in intent and certainly valuable in today's world where people are forever falling prey to low self-esteem, there is a danger. This danger is exemplified by the ancient Hebrew legend of Balaam. According to the legend, Moses was for a time a fugitive in the camp of the King of Ethiopia. The King was in the odd position of besieging his own capital because it had been taken over by the unrighteous sorcerer Balaam, who used his powers to influence others without higher purpose. Balaam represents that part of the psyche that seeks power without reference to anything higher than self-love.[1]

One must, of course, have a degree of self-esteem to tackle the acting world and remain dedicated to spiritual service. The service, however, must be rooted in something higher than the self or one could step across the boundary into what is commonly known as black magic. And as a teacher of mine once reminded me: black magicians die like dogs.

Higher purpose implies something larger, something beyond the small self. It also reiterates the idea that creation is modular—systems are nested within larger systems—and that by changing the frequency of energy fields, we can interact with other systems. Higher purpose, then, is related to contacting and, in some way, serving a larger or higher energy field.

Using Bentov's model, human consciousness is being stimulated to grow to the level where it can allow its sophisticated body of knowledge to be absorbed by a giant information bank. Like cosmic reporters who are reporting *on* the creation *to* the creation which *is* the creator. Or as Shankara, the Indian philosopher, says:

> *On the vast canvas of the Self*
> *the picture of the manifold worlds*
> *is painted by the Self itself.*
> *And that Supreme Self*
> *seeing but itself,*
> *enjoys great delight.*[2]

E.J. Gold's model is the same, only he takes it one step further and suggests that the Supreme Self cannot properly see itself because it has become ensnared by its own creation, forced, as it were, by the whole process to doze. Man's purpose, then, is to awaken the endless creator, the Absolute, by awakening himself and thus alleviating the suffering of the Absolute.

Wait a minute, you say? To do what? Alleviate the suffering of the Absolute? How can the Absolute suffer? Well, that is the bonus question and I'm not going to give my answer and risk stealing your work from you. Suffice it to say that most religions adhere to a notion of God's suffering—the crucifixion of Jesus being the obvious example—in which man has a role to play by either alleviating that suffering or being redeemed by it.

These ideas may be confusing or burdensome at first, I know. And clearly, not everyone is capable or called to participate directly in such service. Some actors can take solace in knowing that their experiences are valuable and their very being is a great and useful contribution to the collective hologram of experiences being assembled by the Absolute.

But for those who can see little joy in life as it is, who want to participate in the struggle for evolution—well, there may be work ahead.

A good way for an actor to begin to discover true higher purpose is by cultivating compassion towards character. Like a puppeteer who has the compassion to animate and give life to something inanimate, the actor can give life to a character, that until the actor breathes life into it, remains nothing but words on a page.

As the character grows, the actor must begin to identify with and actually sympathize with the entire character, even the ugly or negative aspects. This act of opening up to the character, loving it, seeing the flaws and faults, playing the truth of the character unconditionally, is an act of profound compassion. And the foundation for real self-esteem.

To surrender to the character, with no craving for reward, is essential. It can begin the process of dissolving the ordinary need for reward and establish a new frame of reference for work—one that is not dependent on the reward system.

And by doing this, one can overcome Balaam, one can recognize the gifts that already exist and pay the debt to the universe by becoming ready to aid in the work of reunification, also known as redemption.

This service, sacrifice, aid, whatever you want to call it, is the key to establishing higher purpose. Keep in mind that because of the wide variety of souls and paths, your higher purpose may not be suited for anyone else but you. And as such, attempts to convert others are very often a transference of insecurity ("Gee, if I get enough people to believe like me, then I can banish my inner skeptic and feel secure at last").

With dedication and guidance, the actor has the opportunity to resonate with higher entities, accumulate data, and experience the kind of awareness normally reserved for saints and sages. That is not to imply that everyone will do so. In fact, as a result of humanity's slumber,there are very few people who will attempt a path of self-cultivation and fewer still who will manage actually to achieve anything of consequence. Nevertheless, there is hope, and grace, and possibility for actors to serve a higher purpose, and in so doing, to sanctify their art. What are you waiting for?

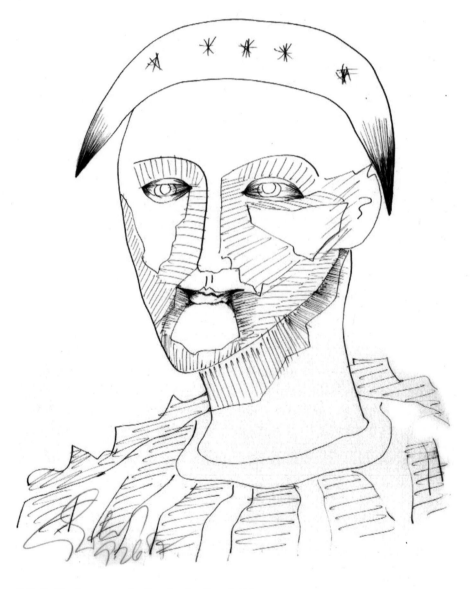

E.J. Gold, *Anatomy of a Troubador,* Pen & Ink,
pencil signed, 11" x 15", Rives BFK,
© 1987 Heidelberg Editions International.

CHAPTER TEN

MINDFULNESS AND ACTING

> To be fully conscious in all situations and conditions of life, is what the Buddha meant when he said we should be mindful while sitting, standing, lying down, or walking. But "fully conscious" does not mean to be conscious of one aspect or function of our body or mind, but to be conscious with and of our whole being, which includes body and mind and something that goes beyond body and mind: namely that deeper reality at which the Buddha hinted in the term "*Dharma*" and which he realized in the state of Enlightenment.[1]
>
> – Lama Govinda

If you have studied acting, the following description may be familiar to you: you are working on a sense-awareness exercise in acting class. Perhaps the teacher has you lie down on the floor and imagine you are on a beach sunbathing. The instructor tells you not to generalize the feeling of the sun on your body, but rather to sense where the exact highlights are and to let that inform your entire instrument. Or how about this one: the instructor asks you just to breathe and simply be aware of the breath going in and out, perhaps saying a poem or a few lines from a play as you do this. Maybe you have been asked to visualize yourself into the atmosphere of one specific place or another. Or if your class is geared to a more active dynamic, the instructor may have you walking around the room, leading with different areas of the body, and observing the feelings associated with the different postures. You may be surprised to know that these and countless other acting exercises are variations of an ancient meditation practice called Mindfulness.

The meditation is associated most often with Buddhism, particularly Japanese Zen, but there are similar practices in almost all religions. The motive for such exercises, in religion as well as in theatre, is to focus the attention. The results vary according to the ultimate aim of the practice. Generally, however, it is to calm the habitual chatter of the mind, train the muscle of attention, and over time to develop authentic insight.

The starting point in most Buddhist-based practices is the mindfulness of breath. The adept sits in a posture that allows the spine to be straight and the balance to be "locked," avoiding any sudden movements or falling. Then the mind rests at the belly, around the navel, and simply watches or, in some cases, counts the breath.

I have experienced this, sitting in zazen meditation every morning for a few years, and although it sounds easy, it is not. The mind wants to scatter. It resists the intention just to sit and focus. The mind is often likened by Eastern teachers, at least, to a group of chattering monkeys in the jungle swinging from one tree to another; thoughts that jump from one subject to another. However, after mindfulness training and with gentle persistence, the mind will surrender to the calm and allow a profound, silent, and authentic peace to spread throughout the being.

Although certainly useful for all people seeking a break from the hyper pace of modern living, mindfulness is particularly helpful for actors. Seated meditations are useful in clearing the mind of cluttering noise and thereby facilitating clarity of analysis, unity of focus, coherent interaction with others, and a relaxed sense of well-being. A similar kind of peace is attained in movement-based meditations such as Tai Chi Chuan. Once the movement sequence is learned, the breath and subtle energy collaborate in a mindful way to create a smooth undisturbed meditation. Tai Chi can help link consciousness from one unfolding moment to the next without breaking the thread of attention. It can help actors to be grounded, to trust a soft, yet powerful, stillness, and in many cases, it can release tension blocks that have become obstacles to full expression. The added benefit of doing Tai Chi is that it generates a healthy life force and maintains the body in a fit, yet flexible, shape.

As with anything, there is a down or shadow side as well. If abused or done without a harmonious lightness, Tai Chi can become an end in itself, keeping the actor ensnared in the form and habituating a single mode of movement. Seated meditation can also become an end in itself, and if not properly prepared, westerners have been known to weaken and even damage their knees and hips.

How then should an actor practice mindfulness? Well, sensible and balanced inclusion of moving or seated meditation is good. However, they are only useful if integrated into your life in a practical way. I took acting classes from the very fine actor, Michael Moriarty, who would from time to time share instructive stories about his own life. In one, he told us how, at one time, he spent two years as a serious student of Zen. He would go to the Zen center in New York and sit, somewhat miserably, in his full or modified lotus position, meditating. Near the end of his time there, still wrestling with the leg and back pains, and wanting desperately to know the truth, he had a thought arise in his meditation that liberated his practice into his work. It was a simple realization really, but very powerful: "I am an actor, and an actor must find truth in all positions."

That freed him from the seated practice and invited him back into the professional application, bringing him back to his craft with renewed vigor. And when he told this story, I, too, was liberated. I, too, realized that all of thses practices are also traps, and at some point, one must be willing to surrender the habit of perpetual seeking and actually find! One can learn from these various Eastern practices, but anyone interested in being an actor, must leave the zafu pillow and engage the world.

There are, by the way, a growing number of very effective Western practices that have slightly less grand asperations than their Easten counterparats, but are enormously pwerful nonetheless. The Alexander Technique, for example, widely used in training actors in Britain, Canada, and the U.S., is very close to being a Zen endeavor. F. Matthias Alexander was a pioneer in the mind-body unity. He developed his theories in the last decade of the nineteenth century and then taught until his death in 1955. It would take volumes to illuminate the breadth of his work and influence, so I will limit myself to a few key elements that are most closely allied with Zen practices.

Alexander discovered that many of the problems plaguing people with regards to their posture or their vocal work stemmed from a habitual misue of the head-neck connection. That area where the spine entered the cranium was of paramount interest to Alexander, and he set about to find ways to release that area and in so doing, liberate better overall balance and sense of well-being. Using a system of guidance dominated by the head-neck connection, he helped many people to find the elegance and flow of the entire body.

While Zen does not necessarily find that connection to be of paramount value, his directions from the student to place the mind at that one area at the back of the neck, while monitoring changes in the interior and exterior, is very close to a Buddhist insight meditation known as Vipassana.

In Vipassana, the meditator places his attention on part of the body, maintaining a gentle but steady focus on that part, staying alert to the changes in awareness.

The meditation has more options, but the two practices are essentially the same. Alexander technique just prefers to focus on the head-neck area.

There are other similarities: in Zen, there is the idea of mastering the balance and awareness in the four basic postures of sitting, standing, walking, and lying down. Initial Alexander work begins with just these same postures. And afterwards, Zen teaches that essential mindfulness and grace should be applied to all activities of the day, regardless how mundane. On this Alexander himself says:

> The essence of the religious outlook is that religion should not be kept in a compartment by itself, but that it should be the ever-present guiding principle underlying the "daily round," the "common task." So also it is possible to apply this principle of life in the daily round of one's activities without involving a loss of attention to these activities.[2]

Being attentive to the postural relationship of the body to gravity, and using thought to redirect habitual patterns of movement, is an activity requiring presence in the moment. The monitoring and re-learning throughout the day create a fresh mental awareness with a graceful physical ease. This is pure Zen.

This is not to imply that the process is entirely without effort. We are creatures of forgetfulness and the effort to *remember* to balance the head and to redirect the actions of sitting, walking, and so on, takes a good deal more fortitude than you might think. The experience of internal composure that accompanies alignment, however, establishes an appetite for that composure and eventually makes the remembering easier.

Another parallel between Zen practice and Alexander technique is the concept of *inhibition*. Alexander used the concept, not in the sense

of thwarting desire or suppression, but in reference to by-passing habitual modes of thinking and doing. He discovered that once the thought
to do something happened, such as deciding to stand from a sitting
position, the nervous system engaged a habitual and highly conditioned
set of nerves, charging them up with a "ready" tone of energy awaiting
the command to act. In most cases, this set pattern was a network of
nerves established with what he called, "The wrong sense of what's
right."

Therefore, in a lesson, the Alexander teacher might tell a student
to tell herself that she is not going to stand—and then to stand up. This
way she inhibits the original impulse to stand, allowing a new pattern
to be learned.

Paul Reps, at the end of his book *Zen Flesh/Zen Bones* includes a
list of practices and meditations. One of them is clearly the directive
of inhibition. It says: "Just as you have the impulse to do something
—stop."

Finally, one of the key elements in Zen is non-attachment, particularly to result. Attachment to result is really the same thing as
Alexander's term, *end-gaining*. Alexander used this concept to
describe people who used their will to hammer their way towards a
desired end, with little or no concern for the means. The end gainer
insists on the process simply "feeling right." The problem here is that
whatever activity the end gainer is doing, he has a misdirected use of
his instrument. Therefore, improvement and excellence is nearly
impossible. Feeling right, in this case, is a deterrent to learning.[3]

As stated earlier, Alexander was a pioneer in this field. Since his
time, there have been an ever-growing number of teachers and
researchers who have advanced the knowledge to a remarkable degree.
Still, Alexander's fundamental techniques are the most widely used,
especially in the world of training actors.

There is another outstanding practice I should mention, and that is
the work of Moshe Feldenkrais. His *Awareness Through Movement*
and *Functional Integration* techniques have made huge contributions
to the field. His work, limited at first to clinical cases, has expanded
out and become hugely successful in helping developing actors. His
work has been enthusiastically endorsed by the famed theatre director,
Peter Brook. In addition, a growing number of theatre schools in
Europe and elsewhere employ Feldenkrais practitioners to help train

their actors.

Sounding very much like a Zen master himself, Moshe once said to those of us attending his workshop in New York: "Even if you absorb all the psychological systems in the world, you will accomplish nothing until you change your relationship to time."

The actor works in the medium of time. Condensed moments, comic timing, pauses, silences, pacing, tempo—these are just a few of the elements of time an actor must master. To master those elements implies being free of them as well. Mindfulness is a method of finding this freedom. In true mindfulness, time is elastic, unfixed, and playful —allowing for freshness, a fluidity that audiences desperately want to experience.

There is a concept in actor training called "moment to moment" and it describes a level of awareness in which the actors agree to live each moment to its fullest. It is a mind-set that can release the natural flow of inner impulses, allowing the actors to experience the unfolding story and unfolding relationship dynamic without the interference of the ego. If it is a play or a scripted scene, the words no longer come out automatically, the way a musician in an orchestra plays the notes when the score demands it. Instead, the notes, or rather the words, come out according to the reality of the situation. They are provoked and cajoled forth and, as a result, each moment is more connected, more vivid, and ultimately, more true.

An actor who progresses to the stage where he or she can fully trust his/her preparation and innate sensibilities will express and experience a radical truth, an artistic and profoundly new relationship to time. Soon, under these conditions of repeated exposure to the creative state, the actor begins to work from the "authentic" self. When that happens the actor taps into a deep wellspring of strength and joy. The moment-to-moment mindfulness of a good actor, just like the exciting improvised riffs of a good jazz musician, can inspire an audience to experience the work with that same rarified level of attention. A successful wave of this riveting form of attention can revive our hope for a better world and alleviate suffering of all kinds, especially the background fears of death and dying. When that shift of attention happens and the events in time seem to be newly-minted in a nowness so sharp, it penetrates into a freshly born reality, we are suddenly reminded that there exists only the eternal now in an infinite here, and that as human beings, we are much more than a walking, talking parade of self-images. As Shakespeare has Prospero say, "We are such stuff as dreams are made on."[4]

Clearly there are exercises and techniques developed in studios through the years that help actors surrender to this mindfulness, this moment-to-moment reality, or the term would not be so prevalent. Even with the crushing layers of conditioning that molds all modern humans and forces them to linger back in reveries of the past or in anxious pursuits of a fantasy future, there are reliable methods to bring actors out of that spell and awaken them into the present moment. Research gleaned from Gestalt therapy and from Zen Buddhism and many spiritual traditions has found its way into the many studios of actor training. All of them are focused on relieving the practitioner of the burden of the ego and allowing them to surrender to the lively present fullness of mind. In some situations this occurs because of an enforced, albeit scripted, confrontation with mortality.

In Buddhism, the practice of *right mindfulness* (called *satipatthana*) has many practices that have been developed over the years. One uniquely powerful practice recognizes that a very real impediment to being fully mindful in the moment is the discomfort caused by the reality of death. The anxiety surrounding the subject is responsible for literally thousands of distractions and destructive tendencies the world over. Therefore, the Buddha created an exercise that is designed to help overcome fear of death by dropping all sensual attachment to the body. To do this, the adept must view his or her own body as a corpse in some stage of decay. She must visualize and consciously face the reality of eventual death and decay. This is the *reflections on the states of the body* exercise and in some sects, their work is enhanced by literally observing the day to day decomposition of a monk who had passed away. This exercise then gives way to the reflection on the states of feeling, the states of mind, and the states of things.[6] These reflections provide profound wisdom and work to loosen the practitioner's hold on the socially accepted consensus reality.

I mention this because there are times in an actor's life when he or she will be called upon to portray dying and death. Meryl Streep apparently went deep into this mystery for a scene in the film *Ironweed*; her work was so true, the crew and the director were actually concerned that she had indeed passed away.[7] Sarah Bernhardt slept in a coffin—no doubt to shed the fear of death and bring life into sharper focus. All of the great actors, and certainly the great classical actors, have had to confront the reality of death. Even a cursory look at any of Shakespeare's plays will reveal that he has people dropping right and left. And, of course, in recent times, the majority of television and film stories have death and dying as a preoccupation.

What perfect opportunities for actors to confront fear of death and to go deeply into it, even as a Buddhist monk would do. These opportunities given to actors are profound meditations in many religious orders, not just Buddhism. The actor has been given the possibility to use these and similar techniques not only to enhance his art, but also to establish his momentum on the spiritual path. This is accomplished, in part, by shedding fears and vanities in order to surrender to a deep and delightful right mindfulness.

An actor wanting to deepen his way of working should consider the mastery of mindfulness. It can be applied in nearly all areas of actor training: postural alignment, breath release/control, timing, physical characterization, death scenes, and the simple awareness of the moment at hand while performing virtually any task. The real beauty of it is that it engenders honest, centered spontaneity—something every actor can put to good use. In mindfulness, then, for the actor, as well as the spiritual adept, the means is the end result.

3.10.89

E.J. Gold, *Heaven and Hell,* Pen & Ink,
pencil signed, 11" x 15", Rives BFK,
© 1989 Heidelberg Editions International.

CHAPTER ELEVEN

GATEWAYS

Our "field" in life, the terrain in which we live and work, is also a specialized window through which we view the world. Actors have the unique opportunity to adopt many points of view over a single lifetime, providing a much wider spectrum of understanding than normally available. These various windows or gateways can, over time, reveal certain aspects of reality that speak to the profound ineffable mystery of life. The craft at this level becomes a religious experience; not in the smiling bake sale sort of way, but as a deep revelatory thrill at the interconnectedness of people, events, history, art, music, life, death, and the beyond. Voluntarily assuming various points of view, if done fully and with complete conviction, eventually erodes the barnacles of prejudice and gently seasons the soul toward compassion and further growth.

That explains why actors now and throughout history have become activists of one sort or another. They come to appreciate humanity on a deep trans-cultural level and come to know their own demons with such intimacy and reward that they see clearer than most how whole groups of people fall victim to their own hardened and repressed demons. Most riveting of all is the knowledge that repressed or disowned demons become projected outward into the environment, distorting the windows of perception and causing extraordinary suffering and violence.

I have thought about this for many years and now, having lived and observed life on this planet for five decades, I see that much of the world's violence and suffering has occurred because of one damnable phrase: "My god's better than your god." Experts as well as aware parents know that the tacit use of this phrase in whatever form, especially if used to bring harm to others, matches the mentality of an emotionally reactive three-or four-year-old child. A child at that age has no conscience and is absorbed in the primal urge to stake personal claims, to resolve the newly experienced vulnerability through a tyrannical self-centeredness. This may be fine in children, because with some guidance they will grow out of it and move on to the next stage of development. When this proprietary claim is expanded and adopted by a group mind-set, it becomes a dangerous scourge upon the entire global community.

Is it the fault of this or that group, this or that country, this or that religion? Of course not, it is merely the stage of development that all individuals, groups, countries, and religions must go through as part of their normal evolution. However, when these various groups in the grip of a four-year-old mind-set get their hands on weapons developed for more evolved and mature minds, a tragedy ensues. Let's face it, most sane, mature people do not give guns to four-year-old children. Yet someone, or rather many people, are happily manufacturing and supplying such toys to these childlike groups every day. Who are these people? What sort of sadistic, greedy mind would supply weapons and ammunition to any group childish enough to indulge in playing "my god is better than your god?"

The adult world community must wake up and instead of simply reacting to horrors and genocidal events occurring across the globe, they must intervene and, if necessary, dismantle the manufacturers and the supply chains that keep the atrocities fueled with weaponry. Look to the adults who are making huge profits from the suffering of others, and the trail will lead to the source. Just as we would find and stop a person who introduced knives into a game of football, we must find and stop a person who is doing essentially the same thing with warring tribes. We cannot expect children to skip stages of growth, but we can protect them from doing harm to themselves and others in the process.

You see, for an actor who has experienced several opposing points of view, it becomes clear that we are all equally wrong and all equally right. It becomes clear that no one perspective has the whole picture and that the human family must place their attention on those transcendent common denominators that highlight our universal experience and, by doing so, a natural appreciation and respect for the cultural differences will emerge. Once this is in place we will no longer be trapped by the childish perspective of "my god is better than your god."

When groups or individuals become trapped in this mind-set, the level of idiocy of this should be obvious to everyone involved. Yet, sadly, it is not. Why not? What would be the harm in making the global assumption that the vast intelligence of the universe with its infinite correlating abilities, infinite timelessness, infinite space, and infinite mind, is capable of manifesting in infinite varieties? Isn't it obvious that we are in a UNI-verse? One God?

And one need not be a seeker long before discovering that the variety of "ways" or "paths" to knowing this one God number in the thousands. Understandably, each path protects its own approach by opposing other approaches. And even within a single approach there are sects and orders that define themselves in opposition to the other sects and orders.

In Christianity, for example, there evolved many branches of faith, even within the original Roman Catholic Church. As a result, there exists a wide variety of orders of monks and nuns who operate in vastly different ways. Christianity further branched out after the break with Roman rule, resulting in an ever-increasing array of Jesus-centered religions.

Similar branching has occurred with every major and minor religious path in the world. It is as if a mathematical equation is at work, an equation that parallels closely the structure governing the growth of trees, families, even ideas. It seems that religion, like nature, follows the route toward increased specialization and refinement.

Also, it is evident that nearly all world religions center around a core figure or hero who either arrives with or attains godlike stature: Jesus, Buddha, Mohammed, Zeus, Moses, Shiva, and so on. Some religions are adamant about their way being the *only* or *right* way. And indeed, the respective Godheads insist on fidelity to their religions. They warn against getting involved with the heathens, pagans, barbarians, cannibals, witches, or devils that inhabit the other houses of worship.

When I was younger, I was greatly repulsed by the "private club" mentality of most religions. Later, as I progressed on my "pathless path," that wonderful life as an actor that exposed me to many points of view, I recognized this separate posture as merely a sealant, a necessary part of all religious orders. As a congregation or group is formed, they become, in essence, a cellular entity. They must create protective membranes to secure the integrity of their structure. The process of doing that, at least in the early stages while dealing with immature new arrivals, often involves the rejection of other cellular structures.

Although this process of self-definition may appear unfair or unnecessary, the simple fact is, it *is* necessary. Why? Because, in the-words of St. Matthew: "Strait is the gate, and narrow is the way, which leadeth into life."

Joseph Campbell, in his televised interview with Bill Moyers, made a lovely modern analogy to describe this very ancient idea. He compared religions to software on a computer. Each personal computer is linked to the main terminal—or God. However, every software program has its own code, and it is only after learning the code that you can eventually access the main terminal, that place where all religions meet. Computer geeks as well as wizened leaders of the various religious cells know that dabbling in software is interesting, but it can't take you very far unless you stay and master one format.

The defining of a method or religion in opposition to other methods, therefore, is really motivated by the knowledge that young seekers are curious, and if they aren't prodded to stay on one course, they will wander off, dabbling in the glittering software market. The fear is that useful and familiar traditions will die, families will split, indigenous ethnic cultures will fall. However, as usual, this essential concept is lost or ignored, and before too long, there are those who fervently come to believe that other methods are not only to be avoided, but are to be hated and even destroyed. This level of ignorance gives rise to great suffering.

The reason people become so monstrous is usually related to the urge to acquire and maintain power, which in turn is related to a deep fear of dying. Again, a childish mind in the throes of fear and denial of death comes to believe that dominance over other humans will in some way secure immortality. In its extreme form, it is the vulnerable child mind-set again, believing that the enforced suffering and death of others gives evidence, by contrast, of a secure life force.

Real power, however, power that is not a projection of the fears of

dying, is a power described by most religions as a true inner peace—
an understanding of one's place in the universe. People who have no
inner peace, who ignore their possible place or suspect that there is not
such a thing, sense a deep weakness or hunger inside that must be con-
stantly bolstered and fed.

I have known performers like this. They must have constant reinforcement of their worth. They are desperate for acceptance and in the
misguided attempt to reduce their desperation, they will often sacrifice
the intimacy that they truly need in exchange for applause. I have also
known others who, for a variety of reasons, confidently knew their
worth. Without resorting to puffery, they could accept the love of an
audience as well as that of friends and intimates.

These performers with real inner power have what is often
referred to as *presence*. There is a noticeable vitality about them. It is
not by chance that famous performers are described as "luminaries" or
"stars." In esoteric terms, they have developed their internal power to
the degree that they can activate what is known as *radiance*.

There are different levels of radiance similar to different levels of
light. The radiance of a "healthy glow," for example, is a low level but
recognizable light. The "after glow" of sexual intercourse is a slightly
higher level light, but still low when compared with the bright light of
sexual union. Some actors beam onstage, others might glow, and still
others, albeit only a few, seem to blast with radiance—one can't stop
watching them.

Many Indian Gurus are said to emit a radiant light. It is believed
to be beneficial just to be in the presence of this *enlightened* energy.
Ram Dass, teacher and author of *Grist for the Mill* and *Be Here Now*,
tells of how his Guru maintained a flow of light that emanated a steady
warmth and love-filled radiance enjoyed by anyone in his immediate
circle of influence. This vibration from an advanced being can work to
elevate the spiritual possibility of an entire community—that is why in
India, Yogis who sit, radiating in deep meditation, are considered a
valuable asset. They are supported with enthusiastic contributions
from the community.

Radiance, especially of the face, is considered by many faiths to
be a sign of spiritual attainment. Taoists, for example, are characteris-
tically methodical in their evaluations. For them, if the facial light is
pure and white, it means that one has attained mental energy and

strengthened one's lungs. If the face is radiant black, one's kidneys are strong and one has benefit from the firmness of one's essences. If the radiance is a strong yellow, the person has pure chi or life force.[1]

In the Bible, there are many examples of radiance. Moses, coming down from the mountain with the two tables of Testimony, showed facial radiance because "he had been speaking with the Lord" (*Exodus* 34:29).[2] And there are many accounts of halos and auras being perceived by ordinary people.

I have had some experience with radiance and have witnessed examples of extraordinary luminescence in some beings. Although I understood radiation and knew of its existence in spiritual circles, imagine my surprise when I read Michael Chekhov's book, *To the Actor*, and discovered that he not only recognized its existence, but was explaining the phenomenon as it relates to acting technique!

Chekhov instructs the student to imagine rays shooting out from different parts of the body. He asks them to fill the space with their radiation, imagining that the air around them is filled with light. Then, to my amazement, he gives further instruction that might be a lecture to Tibetan monks in the Himalayas. He says:

> You must not be disturbed by doubts as to whether you are actually radiating or whether you are only imagining that you are. If you sincerely and convincingly imagine that you are sending out rays, the imagination will gradually and faithfully lead you to the real and actual process of radiating.
>
> A sensation of the actual existence and significance of your inner being will be the result of this exercise. The use of outer expressions alone is glaring evidence of how some actors forget that the characters they portray should have living souls, and that these souls can be made manifest and convincing through powerful radiation.[3]

That hidden aspects of reality can become manifest is one of the most fundamental secrets of mystic science and the cornerstone of nearly all religions. It follows that man's ability to imagine something with sincere faith is a key to actualizing. And to create radiance through imagination further implies that the upper worlds are accessed through the power of visualization and that the upper worlds are responsive to that power and manifest energies in this sphere in accordance with man's thoughts.

Whoa now! Take a breath. That means that we participate in Creation and that our world is, indeed, the product of our strongest beliefs. (In this perspective, John Lennon's song, *Imagine*, is a teaching and not just a song.) If we can access the upper worlds through great dedication and sacrifice, as did all the great saints and sages of the world, what do we access without great dedication and sacrifice?

I am baiting the question unnecessarily. We, of course, access lower worlds. Most of us are conditioned to think of lower as grotesque, menacing, or diabolical. Where, in fact, it is simply lower. We aspire upwards because of the perspective it affords us, but it is not a guarantee of a pathology-free life. To be healthy and functional, one must integrate the lower with the upper, or as philosopher and writer Ken Wilber so aptly describes, we must transcend and include.[4]

Some religions, unfortunately, fraction the being by negating the lower, rejecting or banishing or repressing it in hopes that it can be conquered or destroyed. The problem with this kind of thinking is that it imagines a mountain without a valley, light without darkness, clearly an unrealistic and unworkable premise. Other religions recognize the lower as necessary force, the volcanic engine, if you will, to be harnessed in order to produce higher substances. Still others reconcile the whole concept by pointing out the habits of mind that insist upon absurd concepts such as "higher" and "lower." Regardless the belief system, it is evident to all serious seekers that the human instrument has a correlation to a variety of energies.

These energies can be described as "spaces" or "realms" that reflect those three primary states of consciousness available to the human being that we have already discussed. The first is the gross realm—the hard edged three-dimensional world of daily life. The next one is called the subtle realm—the multidimensional world of dreams and visions. The third one is called the causal realm—the area of pure consciousness, the un-manifest dreamless sleep state, the eternal abode of the absolute Self.

Miracles are results of interfacing between realms. A person saturated with the radiation of cosmic dimensions has certain abilities that—from the perspective of someone unfamiliar with the full spectrum of human potential—will appear to be paranormal or miraculous. In the Hindu tradition, some of the lesser powers manifest as bizarre feats of endurance. The other powers, commonly called *Siddhis*, are by-products of advanced training in transcendental Yoga. Some of the Siddhi powers are clairvoyance, weightlessness, leaving one's body and re-entering it at will, supernormal hearing, and mental telepathy.[5]

The Taoists claim similar powers such as insight into subtle laws of the universe, flying, telekinesis, and control of the forces of weather.

There are other religious claims of great healing powers, walking on hot coals, living to be 200 years old, speaking with angelic beings, and raising the dead—to name only a few. These powers may exist or they may be empty carrots created to lure the adept who is attracted to such things toward a life of self-cultivation that will, in the end, dissolve the attraction.

As far as acting is concerned, there are some definite tangible powers—perhaps not as dramatic as those claimed by some religions, but certainly valuable and verifiable.

The most widely-used power for actors is the power of transformation. To be able to *become* another, to consciously surrender to a different set of rhythms, values, and attitudes, is beyond the normal capacity of most people. There is also the power of animal magnetism, whereby the performer can attract and arouse the audience. The ability to capture and hold the attention of others is another power, as is the ability to visualize imagery so clearly, the audience can actually perceive it. For instance, I once saw the famed mime performer, Marcel Marceau, portray an old man in an attic dancing with his deceased wife's dress. I, and everyone else I spoke with afterwards, perceived him dancing with a *red satin* dress.

The ability to radiate is also a power. This is where warmth and a light seems to shine forth from the person. It can stimulate appeal on many levels and makes for very effective stage presence. Mature actors know how to modulate their radiance in composition with other actors on stage, sacrificing personal favor in the quest for genuine ensemble experience. This serves to maintain harmony among the cast and avoids the blatant self-promotion and recklessness that often hinders younger actors.

It takes wisdom and experience to know just how to play with the right measure of truth, the discretion to know when to use and when not to use one's power. Esoterically speaking, the Biblical phrase "Not my will but thy will be done" certainly applies to all of the esoteric powers. Any and all accumulated powers are stabilized by virtue of strict ethics and the level of service to which they are applied. Walt Disney's *The Sorcerer's Apprentice*, part of the masterful animated feature,

Fantasia, is a whimsical but accurate example of power suddenly gained and wielded without wisdom.

Moses, it is said, put a veil over his face. He screened his inner radiance with the mask of the ego. This served not only to keep coarser levels from entering, but also to prevent his inner light from blinding others.6 This veiling is a compassionate act, because when in the presence of a great being, the discrepancies of one's own nature become heightened by contrast, which can be a very painful experience. For this same reason, a teacher often instructs from behind a veil.

A good teacher is a gateway. There is an old adage that says: "When the student is ready, the teacher will appear." In my experience that saying has certainly proved true. There is also the old adage that says, "seek and ye shall find"—which is also true.

The problem for most people is stepping off the merry-go-round. In the momentum of organic life there seems to be a strange conspiracy against finding the truth about who we are. However, once that obstacle is overcome, or as part of overcoming it, a teacher will appear. When you know who you are, you know what to do.

Of course, no teacher is right for everyone. And there are numerous underdeveloped teachers who often have to be passed through like beaded curtains. Some of these teachers have a function and very often it is merely to establish your level of seriousness and dedication. And there are many qualified and truly enlightened teachers walking the planet. The problem facing all beginning students is learning how to navigate through the difficult and sometimes confusing network of teachers.

Perhaps I can supply a few helpful hints for those interested in pursuing their next level of spiritual and artistic evolution. Keeping in mind, of course, that much of my advice will be useless since each path is completely unique. Nevertheless, here's what I wish to offer:

A teacher should be someone who can catch you in your games, who can challenge your masks (something that is rarely pleasant). The teacher must be accomplished in a tradition; must speak to your soul and not your pocketbook; and, ideally, should be accessible, living near enough for daily visits, if need be.

Of course, there are all levels of teachers performing a variety of functions. Some teachers work to evoke adoration, which is dormant in most people. The adoration of a teacher is actually a *sadhana* or practice until the student is open and mature enough to make the realization that the teacher is a reflection of something greater. At that point, the student is free of his or her attachment and progresses very fast.

Other teachers might be stern, demanding, and almost militant. This type of teacher supplies the will necessary to carry the green student until he or she has developed a will of his or her own. This approach is stoic and appeals to students who need the feeling of intense challenge.

There are other teachers of the trickster variety who are there to prod, confuse, and delight the student with skillful means. In this model, the student occasionally gets glimpses of the radiance of a teacher, but the trickster changes too rapidly for the student to form definite attachments. Eventually the student gives up the rational grasping mode and opens to experiences that are perceived directly by the soul.

Whatever the style, and each teacher will be astonishingly unique, teachers should know the terrain of the spiritual path well enough to guide a student safely to his or her own discoveries. There are some teachers who are teaching for the wrong reasons. They may be satisfying a need for domination over others, they may be hiding from their own failures, or what is worse, they may have hypnotized themselves into believing they are enlightened.

In my experience, true teachers are not afraid of their organic undies. That is to say, they are not struggling to portray a saintly image for the sake of the student. Or if they are, it is because they understand the placebo effect of the robes. They are entirely themselves. They will show compassion and humor when it serves the teaching. They will also test the student's sincerity. But, they will never allow themselves to be the victim of the student's projected images of them. Nor will they abuse their power or display punitive measures of dominance. And ultimately, they defy any and all definitions.

Eventually, each seeker becomes his or her own teacher. However, there is rarely a spiritual path that does not stress the importance of proper guidance, especially in the beginning. Upon finding a teacher, one's personal sense of discernment should be the deciding factor. Keep in mind that many of the great teachers veil their radiance, so you cannot go by their "presence" alone. One good way to aid in

Gateways 123

your discernment is to ask the teacher a question to which you already know the answer. The answer you receive will be a useful measurement.

But why should actors find a teacher at all? Haven't I been suggesting that the spiritual elements are in the art of acting? So who needs a teacher?

Yes, the structures of spiritual development are in the art. However, to learn how to orchestrate those structures with exact knowledge and timing you will need a teacher's help. There is no "generic path" to realization, and there are many distractions. The need for a teacher comes at different times for everyone. Some need it early on, others only much later. But all the signs point to the necessity of a true teacher somewhere along the way.

If you find a teacher who has experience with the craft of acting, well, all the better. Unfortunately, the odds right now are against finding someone with a theatrical background. They are out there, just few and far between. So actors needing advanced spiritual instruction must weave themselves into a tradition far enough to receive guidance while maintaining their personal artistry.

Until a teacher emerges, there is help along the way in other forms. One of these I call "divinatories." They are simply one or more of the scores of methods used to "divine" or give "readings" for seekers. The most widely-known methods are astrology, palmistry, and the Tarot. There are hundreds more, some of them so fantastic as to border on the absurd. Phrenology, for example, is a practice in which a specialist feels the bumps and shapes of the cranium to determine individual aptitudes. There is also Pyromancy—prediction of the future by means of fire; Geomancy—prediction by means of earth; Hydromancy —prediction by means of water; Aeromancy—prediction by means of air; Sternomancy – prediction by means of consultation of the area of the body occupied by the sternum; Stoicheiomancy—divination by randomly opening a book and taking the first paragraph on the page as an answer to an already formulated question; Theriomancy—prediction by means of the movement of animals; Capnomancy—prediction by the movement of smoke, and on and on *ad infinitum*.[7]

I dare say one could take any format, add the suffix "mancy" and voila, you have a system of divination! I'm only partially facetious. You see, our world is holographic—that is, every part is at the same time the whole—and given the ability of the human receptors to access a variety of realms, including the realms outside our world of time, any device can be used for divination.

Personally, my experiences with such matters were in conventional forms. It was a little overwhelming at first to have a "reading" that was so completely on target, I suddenly felt naked and exposed. At the same time it was liberating. Even when events unfolded just as the cards or the astrologer predicted, there were always variations on the basic theme dictated by my free will.

For a beginning actor, divinatory data can bring to light hidden talents and help in career guidance. However, as you begin to know yourself more completely, the need for divination becomes reduced. Life itself becomes divinatory.

For the true seeker, the teacher, the powers, the practices, the group dynamics, divinations—virtually everything presents itself as a gateway. Recognizing when the gates are open, however, is a subtle mastery needing great patience and vigilance. Go slowly, as if your life depended upon it.

Assume for now that we access other worlds or dimensions through the masterful use of various gateways. The question then arises, are we accessed by other worlds as well? Some say we are. In the Sufi tradition, it is taught that we are invoking some entity all the time, unconsciously. These are like a multitude of masks that flicker across the mirror of our being. Most of them have become crystallized by the conformity to social structures. When invoked involuntarily, each one assumes it is master of the house, unable to admit there are other masks just around the corner.

If you want to witness a mask change sometime, just insult someone. That's the easiest device because human vanity is so fragile. I guarantee you will see a flicker and a new mask will emerge, completely unrelated to the previous one. Or even better: try to catch your own masks. The difficulty here is that each mask assumes mastery of the house. The mask that is reading this may indeed vow to be watchful, but before long, a new mask will slip in imperceptibly, and it knows nothing of this vow. The mask that remembers will drift to the depths, only to surface much later when the best opportunities for observation are past.

What is to be done? For the actor, it is easier because he usually works in groups. Group dynamics are such that others can begin to recognize the masks, dissolving their hypnotic power and making them recognizable to you. Also, the necessity to maintain character, to establish a working set of masks for the portrayal of a role will facilitate voluntary participation in the play of one's own masks. Then, at some point, masks can actually be used to climb up or down the energy ladder like a totem pole, accessing various realms and accumulating data, knowing all the while that you are free of them.

When this is accomplished, there is true liberation from all the masks of creation. At this level, one becomes the Golden Buddha, sitting by the river laughing and changing masks with glee, radiating brightly. All things become possible because all realms have merged into the One Being.

E.J. Gold, *Strange Angel,* Pen & Ink,
pencil signed, 11" x 15", Rives BFK,
© 1987 Heidelberg Editions International.

CHAPTER TWELVE

SEXUAL ENERGY AND ACTING

I think it can safely be said that more than a few actors of both sexes have entered the world of acting by way of their quest for romantic love. Most actors realized early on that they were usually more desirable while performing in a show than when they were not. This, no doubt, added additional fuel to their ambitions to improve their craft.

Add to this the fact that some people are rather plain in the light of everyday, but on stage or on camera they glow with a transcendent beauty. Some actors seem to get more virile, more vibrant or sensual as they mature. What is their secret?

It's no secret really. It is just the elusive obvious once again. If you look around today, you will see that the modus operandi for nearly all advertising is sex. What is it the tabloids want most to divulge? Sexual secrets! Everywhere, especially here in the West, there is an extraordinary preoccupation with sex.

Ironically, there is also an extraordinary ignorance surrounding the subject. More often than not, sex is either pure titillation or taboo. And now, with the advent of AIDS, sex has become a medical issue laced with clinical information and fear. An epidemic of enormous proportions has begun to infiltrate humanity. Wisely, people are beginning to screen their partners, take special precautions during sex, and in some cases—abstain altogether.

In the wake of this, love scenes for actors are now even more complex than ever before. In the back of their minds, they now must ask themselves, "Is it safe? ... has this person contracted the disease, and if

so ... what do I do?" This fear, regardless of the evidence that points
to AIDS being transmitted only through very specific means (shared
needles, blood transfusions, and sexual emission) will no doubt continue to loom.

Actors, who consciously or unconsciously have long relied upon
the energy of sex to motivate, elevate, and beautify themselves, are facing a strange dilemma. How do they deal with the new sexual climate
and still maintain the open channel to sensuality, intimacy, and bliss?

The first step is to deal consciously with sexual energy. Most people are either prudish (hoping sexual desire will somehow mind its
manners) or promiscuous (rebelling against prudishness by over-
indulging in sexual passion). Both of these approaches are extremes
that can harm the system and ultimately deter progress in many
spheres.

Those who hope to control their sexual desire through repression
make the unfortunate mistake of fanning the flames by reverse psychology. By virtue of the effort needed to deny the desire, it only sub-
limates and grows stronger, needing again more effort and attention
from both the conscious mind and the unconscious. This cycle, as
Freud points out, if left uninterrupted, can and often does result in psychological leaks, sometimes called neurosis.

At the other extreme, people with an overly active sexual life get
trapped in a cycle of ever-increasing thresholds of pleasure and soon
find that they need more and more stimulation. Typically, this cycle of
lust leads to emotional knots that are terribly complicated. All of this
results in the depletion of vital energies—energies needed to refine,
prepare, and activate the spiritual self.

Remember the old adage, *fight fire with fire*? The ancients knew
what this meant. They knew that spiritual attainment was only possible after the flaming horses of sexual energy were harnessed. Their
secret was to use sexual energy in a conscious manner to enhance their
work on higher spiritual centers. They knew that sexual energy helps
man rise above sexual energy.

How this is done is the focus of a number of spiritual disciplines,
Tantra and Yoga being the most widely-known. Both systems have
undeniable merits and can certainly succeed in the transmutation of
sexual energy to serve higher aims. However, my experience with
Tantra, in its Himalayan form, suggests to me a discipline too complex

to be assimilated by someone who is not a renunciate, fully devoted to the form. Yoga (I refer here primarily to Hatha Yoga, but there are other related forms that could be included as well) is simpler and more accessible. However, I caution some actors, because in some people the focus on breathing can dull their awareness.

So far, for me, the best system is the Taoist system. It is simple, effective, and utilizes sexual energy in a way that is directly applicable to actors. The practices can be done anywhere, without drawing undue attention. Also the Taoist style of energy circulation sharpens the mind and deepens the contact with both the physical instrument and emotional body. And finally, it is non-dogmatic, allowing the actor to practice the techniques without being drawn into complex religious training.

The Chinese system, at least in its non-ceremonial form, is very practical. Taoists value mastery in medicine, painting, calligraphy, martial arts, music, poetry, and dance, all of which may be linked to their tantric system if the adept so desires.

The first part of the format is a meditation technique. The technique is primarily concerned with accumulating "chi" or what we might call "vital force," and then directing that energy along the main energy channels in the body. Typically, the channels are blocked in certain places, making it difficult or impossible for the energy to flow. The meditations are used to gradually open them. Once the chi is flowing freely, circulating at full potential (like the energy of an infant), it can then be directed to awaken the higher power centers of the body. Sexual energy, in the Taoist system, is chi, moving at a greater quantity and speed than normal.

The meditation begins by sitting on the edge of a chair with the feet parallel, legs comfortably apart, also parallel. The spine should be erect with the head centered; the hands clasped palm to palm in a relaxed manner, resting on the upper thighs. The feet serve as a "grounding wire" and should stay planted securely on the floor. There should also be a slight forward tilt of the head, avoiding an energy block at the back of the neck.

Next, allow a few deep easy breaths to settle the system and begin to focus the mind. It is good to shake out any tension spots. Then, after the mind has settled a bit, send the intention to allow the mind to rest at the navel. The intention should be effortless. You can aid the process at first by placing your index finger on the navel to help focus the energy. Visualize the navel. And as an added visualization, if needed, see the navel as the center of a target and gradually see the circles of the target shrinking, getting smaller and smaller, moving inwards toward the red innermost circle at the navel.

Rest there momentarily until you feel a warm current of energy. Next, gently intend the current two inches down from the navel to the spot called the *Tan Tien*. This will have a slightly different sensation associated with it and usually deepens the meditation. After a few moments, take the energy to the base of the penis for men and to the ovaries for women. Here, the energy tends to heat up considerably. Next, take the energy to the perineum, the place between the sexual organs and the anus. Once the energy has collected, send it down the back of the legs to the center spot behind the knees, then to the bottom of the feet, then to the tip of each big toe, then back up the outside of the legs to the points behind the knees, and return to the perineum.

At this point, there are options for further circulation that should be done only after competent guidance from a meditation instructor. For now, allow the energy to return step by step to the navel center where it can be stored.

This meditation is known as *The Microcosmic Orbit* and is often taught at Tai Chi centers or Taoist Esoteric Yoga Centers in most major cities. Mantak Chia, one of the leading advocates of the system, has written a number of excellent books on the various disciplines. His book, *Awaken Healing Energy Through the Tao* (Aurora Press), is the best book on the meditation techniques I have come across. Also, women may want to read his book, *Cultivating Female Sexual Energy* (Healing Tao Books), for more specific information regarding the meditation as it applies to women.

Overall, the meditation takes 15 to 20 minutes and does not require a lotus position of the legs or special pillows or mantras or anything but concentration. Let me also remind you of Michael Chekhov's point regarding the power of imagination. You need only visualize and imagine the energy traveling and, in a short time, the energy will begin actually to flow. I can say personally that when the energy began to circulate in my body and I began to direct it to specific points, it dramatically improved my awareness of energy channels not only in me, but in others as well.

In addition, I have maintained a healthy and youthful constitution due to my daily practice. It has been suggested that the fabled "fountain of youth" that so many early explorers were seeking, is none other than the fountain of energy, the current that is developed within the body through this practice. In addition to promoting youthful vitality, the meditation helps to balance blood pressure, improve digestion, regulate sleep, and clarify and enhance all of the senses.

This meditation is the preparatory meditation for the advanced version that is used in Tantric sexual practices. The energy of both partners begins to circulate in a manner that magnifies the sense of communion, reduces the usual quick race to a climax in favor of a much more profound and pleasurable and long lasting bliss. The woman experiences greater ecstasy over a much longer period of time, the male learns to control ejaculation and circulate the vital energy in a manner that retains fluids and maintains desire.

Couples who have interest in this can consult some of the books out on the subject. Master Da-Love Ananda, in his book, *The Eating Gorilla Comes in Peace*, has a chapter on the subject. In it he states:

> When the couple separates, the male should commonly or frequently retain an erection, and the female should remain full of life and even desire. The remaining desire and fullness is our advantage, our true food ... such fullness is itself a means of attracting more life, whereas exhaustion or conventional degenerative satisfaction only provides a means whereby we are emptied of life in every moment of living.

And later in that same chapter:

> The regenerative process does not eliminate the orgasm; it transforms the orgasm. Thus, the response that would otherwise produce the orgasm must continue to be present in sexual communion. Through right participation in the ecstatic or overwhelming pleasurable response, something occurs in the body that is regenerative and that serves the awakening of the higher functions of the brain.[1]

In the tradition of Tantric Yoga (Tantra meaning "method"), there are *asanas* or *Yogic Postures* specifically designed for sexual union. These postures help to channel the energy along exact routes with a force so powerful it will liberate what is called *Kundalini* or *The Psychic Current*.[2] However, Tantrism (at least for Westerners not raised in Indo-Asian traditions) is highly ritualistic, and as I've stated before, somewhat impractical for western actors.

In my experience, extensive ritual is not necessary to master the breathing, postures, *ejaculation control*, or any other parts of the practice. Others I have spoken with agree that it is largely a matter of knowing it is possible and then applying a few techniques. The only obstacle to this becoming a widely known practice is the same obstacle to all spiritual practice, namely ignorance. People are reluctant to sacrifice the instant roller-coaster thrills of their habitual existence in favor of the slower, more subtle and more truly sacred pleasures. What they do not realize is that these subtle pleasures are keys to unlocking energy reserves of immense power that are then used to serve true purpose and meaning in life. And considering that possibility, what could be a greater thrill?

Actors of all ages and types can begin to capitalize on their own connection to Eros, that blissful delight accompanying sexuality, and in so doing come to know and partake of the greater cosmic dance of Eros. The vitality, wisdom, and perspective they gain will inevitably enhance their lives both onstage and off.

E.J. Gold, *The Matador's Woman,* Pen & Ink,
pencil signed, 11" x 15", Rives BFK,
© 1987 Heidelberg Editions International.

CHAPTER THIRTEEN

NOT ME—NOT NOT ME

Through preparation and refinement, the actor can invoke high spiritual energies in the roles of gods, heroes, and saints. The actor can invoke slightly lower energies in the form of struggling or non-struggling mundane humans. Slightly lower we see clowns, buffoons, and idiots. Lower still, we see cruel murderers and violent, ugly people. Even lower we meet demons, gargoyles, and beasts.

The actor is there to show us how we are usually entranced by life, helplessly invoking a confusing array of energies and becoming the pawns of our own powers. At the same time, the actor demonstrates through the act of acting the ability of humans to cease unconscious identification with the energies by taking conscious control. This gives hope for humans to be able to dehypnotize themselves from their compulsive, limited views. It further establishes a means to respond to their higher aims.

In his book, *Between Theatre and Anthropology*, acclaimed theatre researcher and director Richard Schechner says:

> We might even say that there are two kinds of transportations, the voluntary and the involuntary, and that character acting belongs to the first category and trance to the second. However, having watched trance—and having seen many films depicting it—I suspect that the differences between these kinds of transportations have been overemphasized. The character actor is self-starting (at least if he has orthodox Euro-American training), but once warmed up and in the flow of things, he is deeply involved in what Keats called the "negative capability," and what I've schemed out as the "not me-not not me." The character actor in flow is not himself, but he is not not himself at the same time. Also, trance performers are frequently conscious of their actions even while performing them; and they too prepare themselves by training and warm-up.

The difference between these kinds of performance may be more for labeling, framing, and cultural expectations than in their performance process.[1]

Like a chant or a mantram or a koan, the actor's repetitions of the script and of the voice and postures of the intended character, during the development of rehearsal period, work on the telepathic circuits of the brain. In a moment similar to states in meditation, an actor feels a shifting or a clicking in and the character seems to be fully there. Robert De Niro, Meryl Streep, Daniel Day Lewis, and others are famous for their abilities to "plug in" as it were to their characters. They mold a psychological point of view, enter into a framework of physical and vocal energy, creating a working persona, and then leap into a moment-to-moment secondary reality.

Like the character created by an actor we all have formed our own working persona through socialization, gratification of sensual pleasures, and dependence on others. Every situation in life at some point calls forth the appropriate mask, automatically and uncontrollably. The real self will eventually recognize the discrepancy between its wishes and the tyranny of the masks that make it feel trapped. This is the beginning of despair.

The Buddha declared that one of the primary sources of our human despair was the belief in a fixed self, which according to his doctrine does not indeed exist. He hoped to teach others about the beingness that precedes the construction of the selves.

Personality was perceived by the Buddha as a conglomerate invocation of masks. If that is so, then who is wearing the masks? According to the Buddha—we are all Buddhas, temporarily hypnotized by the magnetism of our masks.

Like fighting fire with fire, the actor whose essential self recognizes the dilemma can fight masks with masks. He can consciously invoke his masks, going deeper into the process until he has no fixed persona.

En route, one must find the inner master, the one who is conscious of the changing masks. The source of truth and the strength to face life without a mask comes from this master within.

One way to begin contacting the master within is to use a form of channeling I call the *inner improv*. Getting to the liberating aspect of the master is like peeling an onion. Layer upon layer must be experienced and the peeling process is not altogether enjoyable. This exercise is designed specifically for actors and can be especially useful for actors who have had contact with a spiritual teacher.

At first, it is a free-form experience. I suggest creating a workspace that evokes a special atmosphere. This could be as simple as clearing a room or putting candles on a table. Whatever works. It need not be solemn. It is a way of focusing your point of view.

Next, place about the room in various locations books that are inspirational to you. Also put a few notebooks around with pens next to them. Put a few special garments in various places. These garments should represent qualities of "the master." And finally, create a throne or power place where you can sit or stand and speak from your heart of hearts.

Then, having cleared two to three hours uninterrupted time in the space, knowing also that you cannot be overheard by anyone, begin to improvise. Walking about and rambling out loud at first will start the ball rolling. Picking up an inspirational book and reading from it at random further focuses the event and keeps the thoughts flowing in the right direction.

Remember to be playful, allowing yourself to be as outrageous as you want. Also remember, you are searching for the "master" within yourself, the one who knows, so be sure to ask questions. When an answer starts to come, be attentive to where it comes from.

Be careful not to preconceive the master character. Keep in mind that a master need not be entirely stern or always of the same sex. Experiment with master characters who are demanding or funny or provocative or even silly at times. Let many manifestations come to the surface. Edit nothing!

Out of these free-form sessions will begin to emerge a character or several characters that speak from a very deep place within you. They will sometimes startle you with their lucidity and insight. And very often they will have unusual and highly unique mannerisms. When you get to this stage, begin to keep a tape player going with plenty of blank tapes to use.

For actors who have studied with a master teacher, it sometimes happens that the teacher's mannerisms and voice can be mimicked until the teacher seems to be speaking through you. Of course, what has happened is those manifestations have unlocked the inner master that the teacher represents to you.

As always, discovering what you do know brings to light what you do not yet know. The inner master can help to clarify intentions and with the new found vision of what needs to be learned help to formulate a true aim. By this I mean formulating a plan of what needs to be done to discover what remains unknown.   Then, once the plan is clear, a personal vow (a deep unbreakable vow) is made to carry out the plan for the benefit of all sentient beings. Having an aim will galvanize the resources of your soul and greatly enhance your chances of evolving in this life.

E.J. Gold, *Dreaming About the Stars,* Pen & Ink,
pencil signed, 11" x 15", Rives BFK,
© 1987 Heidelberg Editions International.

CHAPTER FOURTEEN

WORDS OF WARNING

Like most people in the West, my model of the universe was constructed according to those precepts that can easily be communicated to a child: obey the ten commandments, be good and believe in God, and heaven will await you where you and all your loved ones will be able to live forever. Of course, in adolescence, when my rational mind saw the inadequacy of the child's version and confronted the fear and ignorance surrounding the issue of the human adventure, I became cynical and joined the popular stance that there was no existence beyond death. We live, we die, and that's that.

Then, after a number of extraordinary experiences, the nature of which convinced me that reality was more than what met the eye, and certainly more than what met the eyes of most of my teachers in school, I decided I'd have to educate myself.

Drawing away from the consensus point of view gave me new eyes. I began to see the desperation in the faces of adults who seemed to be running, trying to escape something. I saw gaping holes in our knowledge of reality and wondered why, even after all this so-called evolution, there was such rampant stupidity in the human race.

And then I wondered about heaven. I tried to imagine being totally happy sitting on a cloud in heaven and it irked me. When I began to ask questions, I soon discovered to my great dismay that nobody knew what was going on or what we were supposed to be doing here on this planet. No one had any real data regarding the afterlife.

Gradually, and after considerable faltering and bumbling, I was led to sources that helped me to understand what the poets and mystics were trying to communicate. Even a few of the biblical tales began to make some sense. I was guided from teacher to teacher, weaving in and out of theatre and various spiritual paths until a tapestry of truth began to form. As part of this, I came to know with undeniable clarity that nothing is as it seems. To step into the world of spiritual evolution is to step through the looking glass into realms where the rational mind has no foothold.

Everyone recognizes that the spiritual path is all about transformation. But, most people don't realize the amount of work needed to transform. It takes courage and fortitude to awaken. That is why I have chosen to include a few words of warning. That way, when things get dicey, you can't say I didn't warn you.

The foundation of spiritual fortitude is energy. It takes a lot of it to sustain one through the trials and tribulations of the path. That is why it is important to start early in life; later on, despite all the best intentions, there may not be the energy to accomplish anything.

Also, let me warn you, not only are things not what they seem and great resources of energy are needed, but there are sacrifices that must be made. Not of the bleeding goat variety, although that would seem easier at times. I mean of the personal and very basic kind. For an actor, ambition and personal gain are, perhaps, the first to go.

Conventional ideas of success will be sacrificed as well. The idea of "making it" must not be allowed to dominate the energy charge of the body. Instead, a new flow of energy that *makes it in every moment* will emerge. The fame and fortune carrot will dissolve in favor of the *feast of the now*.

The fixed self-image will have to be sacrificed. The courage to enter new avenues of learning, to risk looking foolish, and to give up the need to be treated as special are all a part of this.

Friends and family are often sacrificed. Not cruelly, but they must not deter you from formulating an aim and sticking to it. Very often friends will feel uneasy and confused if your search takes you in directions contrary to their own experience. It is wonderful and very validating to have support from friends and family, and they must be given ample time to adjust as you explore the inner and outer world options. Yet, when all is said and done, you must walk the walk and must define your path regardless of the protestations. Any real spiritual awakening will return you to them with full embrace and ease and wisdom well worth the waiting.

There are preparations and appropriate timing in the sacrifices, and they differ from tradition to tradition. All seekers, for example, start by sacrificing peace of mind. The search for excellence and the struggle to be a good wellspring guarantees a mind that is on fire, an ecstatic and inspired fire, to be sure, but far from peaceful. The sacrifices clear the heart of the clinging devices of the lower self and allow the being to transcend to the next higher level. Each level, by the way, has its own levels of sacrifice. Including, ultimately, the sacrifice of the powers that may have been accumulated along the way.

The character of the various sacrifices, plus the continuous focus of attention used in acting, the refinement of the nervous system, the radiation of audiences, and proper instruction, can lead one to the brink, the breaking point, or what in the Sufi tradition is known as *The Corridor of Madness*.[1]

You see, part of the problem with humanity is the fact that we are wired wrong. The polarity between the head brain and the sacral (sacred?) nerve ganglia at the base of the spine was somehow reversed. This usually happens early in childhood and is probably a result of the shift from God's will to self-will. The result is a head brain that wants to do all the mentation and the tail brain that tries to command the movements of the body.

Through a variety of means, seekers work to return the reversed polarity to its original form. This is the famed *rising of the Kundalini energy*. What most adepts aren't prepared for is the transition period. This is a state of being produced by the process of re-polarization. It is neither the consciousness of before, nor the consciousness that will be there after the transition. It is the state of being "shattered" by divine energies where the beliefs and mental constructs of the past are breaking down through the non-dualistic truth of the heart. From the outside, it appears as total lunacy. For a detailed and fascinating account of this phenomenon, read Gopi Krishna's *Kundalini*, Shambhala Press, 1971.

As a result, there is a new movement in psychology called *Psychosynthesis*, a form that is developing methods of helping people through this difficult stage of development. Years ago, people in this condition would have been diagnosed as simply psychotic and treated accordingly. But this is changing. Some people are beginning to see the disintegration phase as necessary for a successful reintegration. In

his book entitled *Psychosynthesis*, Roberto Assagioli, the leading pro-
ponent of the movement says this:

> Man's spiritual development is a long and arduous journey, an adventure
> through strange lands full of surprises, difficulties, and even dangers. It
> involves a drastic transmutation of the "normal" elements of the personality, an
> awakening of potentialities hitherto dormant, a raising of consciousness to new
> realms, and a functioning along a new inner dimension.
>
> We should not be surprised, therefore, to find that so great a change, so
> fundamental a transformation, is marked by several critical stages, which are
> not infrequently accompanied by various nervous emotional and mental trou-
> bles. These may present to the objective clinical observation of the therapist
> the same symptoms as those due to more usual causes, but they have in reality
> quite another significance and function, and need very different treatment.[2]

One recent example of the corridor of madness was divulged by
André Gregory, theatre director and title actor in the two-person film
by Louis Malle entitled *My Dinner With André*. In the film he goes into
great detail describing a time in his life that was full of inexplicable
synchronicity, hallucination, and wild uncontrollable behavior resembling schizophrenia. He thought he was truly going crazy, only to discover later that it was a spiritual transformation process he was going
through.

Another example is mentioned in *The Asian Journal* by Thomas
Merton, the Trappist contemplative monk. In it he tells of an interview
he had with Kalu Rinpoche, in Tibet. During part of the discussion
about the initiation of Tibetan hermit monks, the Rinpoche tells him
about a period in the two-year dzogchen contemplation when the initi-
ates must encounter and contemplate the "terrifying deities."

We are all familiar with the inspired madness of painters like Van
Gogh, Salvador Dali, or Mark Rothko. We listen with awe to the com-
positions of Beethoven, Mozart, or Stravinsky, read the poetic insights
of Emily Dickinson, William Blake, or James Joyce, and marvel at the
inventions of great sculptors, architects, and even rock stars. Artists
from all ages tend to go to the edge of their consciousness and lean into
the corridor of madness, hoping not to fall. Some fall and some do not.
They all, however, if capable, bring us glimpses of their vision.

St. John of the Cross, one of the greatest Christian mystics,
entered the corridor and wrote of his experiences in his book, *The Dark
Night of the Soul*. In it he gives some directives on how to cope with
the various stages. One of the first is an explanation of why such a corridor exists:

... If a soul aspires to supernatural transformation, it is clear that it must be far removed from all that is contained in his sensual and rational nature. For we call supernatural that which transcends nature, so that the natural is left behind. The soul must completely and by its own will empty itself of everything that can be contained in it with respect to affection and volition, in such a way that, regardless of how many supernatural gifts it receives, it will remain detached from them and in darkness. It must be like a blind man, finding its only support in dark faith, taking it as its guide and light, and leaning upon none of the things which it understands, enjoys, feels, and imagines. And if the soul does not make itself blind in this manner, remaining in total darkness, it will not attain to those greater things which are taught by faith.

Note his insistence on detachment, even from "supernatural gifts." Later he gives more specific warnings against attachment to mystical events that might otherwise seem all too important:

... [S]piritual persons not infrequently experience the presence of forms and figures that are representations of persons from the life beyond, such as apparitions of certain saints, of angels and demons, or certain phenomena of light of extraordinary splendor.

... He then, who has a high regard for such sensed phenomena errs greatly and places himself in great danger of being deceived. To say the least, he will block his way to spirituality. For, as we have stated, there exists no proportionate relationship between all these corporeal things and the things of the spirit .... The reason for this is that if God produces any corporeal vision or any other sensory perception, or if He wishes to communicate Himself to the inwardness of the soul, the effect is felt in the spirit instantaneously, without even giving the soul time to deliberate whether to accept or reject such communication.

Throughout his book he relates a progression along the corridor, full of warnings and advice. Near the end, he talks about the soul walking securely through the darkest parts because it is free of diversions:

The sensual and spiritual desires are now put to sleep and mortified so that they can no longer enjoy the taste of any Divine or human thing; the affections of the soul are restrained and subdued so that they can neither move nor find support in anything; the imagination is bound and can no longer reflect in a rational manner; the memory has lost its strength; the understanding is in darkness, unable to comprehend anything; and hence the will too, is in aridity and constraint...It is in this kind of darkness that the soul, according to its own words, travels securely. For, when all these operations and movements are arrested, it is evident that the soul is safe from going astray. And the deeper the darkness is in which the soul travels and the more the soul is voided of its natural operations, the greater is its security.[3]

It is possible to work alone, to progress steadily amid the chaos of the world. At some point, however, it may become necessary to find help. And be forewarned, once the corridor is entered, there is no way out except by way of the other end. Early exits from the corridor almost always end in madness. That is why guidance and help during this major transition stage is such an important function of a mystery school.

Yet, even within the relative security of a school, there are, from time to time, casualty cases, people who entered the corridor only to lose their way. This is rare, but a possibility and a risk nonetheless.

The sixties saw a great number of casualties due to the indiscriminate use of psychoactive drugs and Yogic practices. Fortunately, the escapist motive has dwindled somewhat in seekers, and that contributes to a more responsible approach to spiritual work.

Therefore be forewarned. The spiritual path is not for dilettantes. An actor of great depth and dedication can recognize that part of himself that occasionally calls out for mediocrity, whispering things like "oh, it'll do" or "we'll live with that." As it is fatal to the artist, so too those whispers are fatal to the seeker. *Getting by* is simply unacceptable.

And know from the outset that although spiritual practices may enhance certain aspects of one's art, they do not supplant hard work and true aptitude. One must not make the mistake of adopting a spiritual quest in order to fulfill artistic ambition. Spiritual progress does not automatically make a good actor.

Also, beware of *spiritual pride*. This is common in young seekers who do not know enough to know how much they don't know. They often give "expert" advice to friends and family without the slightest notion of the consequences. In some, the pride manifests as the exaggerated mask of humility; their outward presence is completely humble, but inwardly they strut with pride and self love.

Beware also of turning spiritual practice into parlor games. Those people who like to dabble in such matters are meddling in areas where they do not belong. The actor is a vehicle, a tuning fork, if you will, and must assume a responsible position by studying slowly and carefully under the appropriate guidance.

Books that encourage indiscriminate healing for the sake of healing or astral projection for the sake of astral projection (or worse, for the sake of science), for example, do so out of naïve enthusiasm for those powers. Unfortunately, they are dangerously ignorant of the consequences and aims of such powers.

My advice, again, is to find authentic instruction. The old adage, *seek and ye shall find*, still holds true. There are guides and teachers available. One's perceptions and readiness will lead one to the guide most suited for the particular stage of development. Then the journey can begin with a secure foundation.

One final word of warning: In Itzhak Bentov's book, *The Cosmic /Comic Book*, he develops an equation that warns of developing *Will* before *Love*. I agree. One's love nature should be strong and unsentimental, providing the steering force for the will. The development of true love through sacrifice, service, devotion, prayer, contemplation, or whatever means, can then direct the will as it develops to serve the highest aims. If done the other way, one risks being seduced by the powers and falling prey to the lure of personal gain.

The world is full of men and women of power, who abuse their power for political or social gains. These black magicians often do not recognize their abuses. They assume that their power is a God-given right. True spiritual transcendence, however, is generated from love (real love, not sentimental love) and in directions unconcerned with temporal power. Let your true heart feelings be the guide.

E.J. Gold, *Arlequine,* Pen & Ink and Pastel,
pencil signed, 11" x 15", Rives BFK,
© 1987 Heidelberg Editions International.

CHAPTER FIFTEEN

PRACTICAL EXERCISES

Performing vs. Acting

Before embarking upon practical exercises, it is important to understand the difference between performing and acting. Most actors enter their training and have production experiences that do not discriminate between performing and acting. Young or inexperienced actors who are not aware of the differences that exist between these two forms of expression, often suffer confusion and frustration for many years as they work to build and establish their careers. They make poor choices in auditions and then, if they get cast, often waste time pursuing inefficient or ineffective approaches to the roles.

It is shameful that so many teachers and programs fail to provide this most important piece of information. It is tantamount to allowing art students to enter the marketplace with the impression that watercolors and sculpture are the same. Granted, they share certain artistic fundamentals and may even be used to express similar or identical ideas, but they are, nevertheless, distinctly different; operating under very different rules and appreciated from very different perspectives.

Acting and performing have much in common, yet, like the visual art forms mentioned above, they are distinctly different and should be treated as such. Performing is more closely allied with those expressions that highlight extraordinary use of the self. Dancers, singers, comics, impressionists, acrobats, jugglers, magicians, musicians, mimes, and all other expressions that are designed to showcase specific talents or to impress the viewer with the extraordinary feats of the performers involved, belong to the world of performance.

Acting is different. It is an attempt to live truthfully within imaginary circumstances. In acting, all performance elements are at the service of maintaining the imaginary world. If there is singing to be done, it is within a specific context such as a lullaby, a serenade, or any other context that allows the actor to sing in character and with a specific intention without it becoming a musical showcase event. If there is dancing, swordplay, juggling, fire-eating, or any other performance attribute that is being expressed, it can be considered acting only if it occurs as a bona fide expression of the character within the given circumstances. Moreover, and this is the key element that will be explored in depth in numerous exercises provided below, it occurs as a bona-fide tactic linked to an action. (In this context, the word "action" has a very exact definition unique to the craft of acting.)

Early forays into acting for most people were usually laced with a variety of reward systems unrelated to the craft itself. Some find they love the attention, certain people crave the social interaction, some find an escape from their lives, and nearly all beginners want and desperately need approval. Due to the nature of the acting game, beginners are almost universally hungry for approval from an audience. They cannot help but see the productions and their performances from the audience's point of view. In many cases, the supportive approval of audiences, particularly those composed primarily of friends and family members, become a drug-like addiction. Before long, the actor will have created both conscious and unconscious strategies to ensure the arrival of that gushing approval fix again and again.

All young children will stand on the edge of the diving board or on their bicycle, horse, skateboard, or what have you, and yell, "Mommy, Daddy, look at me!" The child in us wants to be seen, wants to be applauded for our fabulous feats. It comes as no surprise to learn that most actors still feel that burning desire to be discovered, to be seen by Mommy and Daddy and anyone else who might contribute to their sense of well-being. While somewhat magnified in actors, this trait is quite natural and, if kept in balance, is usually of no great concern.

No concern, that is, until those early strategies developed in childhood cause the actor habitually to shift into performance mode, to distort himself and his onstage reality in order to get the attention, to stand out and to be celebrated for his bravura acting. In this instance, the actor has made a very subtle shift whereby he begins pretending to pretend. In order to insure success, he begins to orchestrate his stage time the way a composer might write a musical score. In extreme cases, he develops false selves that give him permission to interact publicly with elaborate behaviors and soon become subject to fantasy-based self-image problems. What should be a joyful and fulfilling life can and often does descend into a bitter and frustrating cycle of self-aggrandizement and self-loathing.

However, when the actor re-orients the view of the craft and genuinely approaches his work from the point of view of the character and not the audience, joy returns, energy is balanced, and a renewed warmth, security, and assurance pervades the actor's work. This re-orientation is vital. It resolves narcissistic tendencies, allows deep relaxation to occur, and liberates the actor from the mistakes of the past.

It takes time to master real acting and to relinquish performance habits. Some people, however, realize that they are performers and choose to work within the rules and expectations of that form. There is nothing wrong with this. We all love and adore good performers and celebrate them in numerous ways. Some even manage to cross over back and forth between their performing career and their acting. Some manage to blend the two successfully, creating public personas that can be showcased in certain venues. But for those people dedicated to acting, the truest satisfaction comes from succeeding in bringing forth a secondary reality that becomes more potent and vivid than the first.

By distinguishing between performance and acting while simultaneously acknowledging and honoring them both, an actor is given more options, more freedom, and a more reliable relationship to whatever material is being produced. This can enhance all levels of an actor's life and can return the actor to a place of joy and fun, not to mention the eventual fulfillment of her true potential.

What follows is a series of practical exercises. Some are performance-based, some are acting-based, but in keeping with the theme of this book, all of them are designed to give direct experiences of where spiritual work and acting intersect. They should be approached with lighthearted simplicity, focus, a sense of adventure, and if possible, experienced in groups of five or more.

Some of these exercises will warrant informal post-exercise discussion. This serves to assimilate further the experience and to put it into perspective. Please take care to allow all opinions to be expressed, allowing all points of view to be heard and honored. Remember that some exercises are time-released and will only begin truly producing results sometime afterwards.

These exercises are events having the potential to awaken profound and life-altering insights. Therefore, do not rush from one to the other. Stay with one until you feel you have either individually or as a group gleaned all that you can from it at this stage in time.

Some of them need more space than others, but all of them require a clean, secure work environment.

A number of the exercises are geared toward the individual and are designed for very individual discoveries. Others are geared toward a group dynamic, needing an ensemble spirit to link the experience to its intended outcome. In either case, they should be done gently, without pressure to arrive at a predetermined result.

When working in a group setting, it is important that someone act as the facilitator, providing guidance and feedback as needed. All members of a work group or a company should make a pact to leave personal problems or work-a-day concerns outside the chamber until the exercises have reached their end and the session or rehearsal has come to a close. It does no good to enter an exercise if one or more people fail to surrender fully to the demands. Commit to each exercise, and then, only afterwards, following a truly committed experience, will you be in the position to evaluate its effect on you and its value to your work.

It is important to note that these exercises are densely-packed, that is, they can be done over and over again in numerous variations and will continue to reveal deeper and deeper layers of truth, humor, and meaning. Finally, borrowing the words of one of my esteemed teachers: If you aren't having fun, you are doing it wrong!

Sneak Attack

This is a fun variation of a standard improvisation exercise. Here's what happens. Two people enter into a simple improvisation. They must have established answers to the big five questions: Who, What, Where, When and Why. In other words, they need to decide upon who they are and what their relationship is, where they are and when this is taking place (time of day, month, year, and so on), and why they are speaking to one another. This last one is tricky because if it isn't a scene with high personal stakes, the need to talk will soften and eventually fall away.

Next, another actor stands ready, and when the other two least expect it, the third actor enters their scene with a radically different set of the big five. The first two must deal logically and rationally with this invasion and the third actor must remain true to his subjective criteria. The goal is for the scene to find its way to a resolution that seems satisfactory for all three characters.

This can be very funny, but the actors must remain absolutely serious, responding and behaving with absolute sincerity and honesty. If any one of the group begins to play into the comedy and invent wildly, the bottom will drop out and the scene will collapse.

Another version of this same exercise is to have an actor do a sneak attack on a scene from a play. In this scenario, two actors are working on a well-known scene, one that they take pleasure in doing and one that has a distinctive atmosphere. The third actor will knock at the door, crawl out from under the bed, drop in from the window, or any number of methods of arrival and begin to relate to the characters with his or her own agenda. The two actors in the scene must remain in their world and deal with this new arrival using the logic and means appropriate to their characters and their play.

Positive Sabotage

This is less an exercise than a way of approaching a rehearsal to allow more dimension in the work. During a scene in a play or for studio purposes, one or more of the actors make the conscious decision to go about their business, staying true to the text and to the intent of the playwright, but they add to the mix a new and very powerful positive intention towards their acting partner.

While doing the scene, choose to make your partners laugh or to make your partners feel good about themselves, or to make your partners feel uniquely valued or to know how wonderful they are. It is important not to reveal what you have chosen as your sabotage. The other actor or actors need not know anything of this rehearsal technique, but you will find that it propels you further into the work and opens you to fresh moments of communication. Using these and any other positive choices, you, the actor, invest in the other actor in ways that can very quickly boost the level of truth in the scene and set up an appetite for more vivid communication.

Child's Eyes

The leader may participate in this one as long as someone watches the time. Allow a full half-hour for this exercise. It is best done in silence. Because of the nature of the interaction, this one is useful in "bonding" a group, especially before a rehearsal or performance.

To start, have everyone stand in a relaxed, centered posture and gently pat their relaxed "tummy." Use the image of the two-year-old tummy, open and unguarded. Then have everyone massage their own tummies clockwise with the palm of their left hand flat on the belly and the right hand on top of the left. (In this instance, clockwise means if you look down at your own belly, the 12 is just below the navel while the six is just below the sternum). Have everyone sigh long easy breaths to further drop the belly.

There may be some reactions such as giggles or yawns; this is fine during the early stage and perfectly normal as each person lets go of his or her tensions. Later as everyone continues to relax, the faces should open and stay free of expression as people get in touch with their open two-year old mind. As this begins to happen, everyone should simply look about the room, enjoying colors and textures.

Next, they should begin to walk with an easy gait, not trying to "put on" a toddler walk, just walking simply, experiencing gravity as if it were new. Gradually they should begin to encounter one another and look into each other's eyes. When this begins, it is important for the leader to do a bit of side coaching.

Quietly the leader reminds them to keep their tummies soft and relaxed; if they perceive any tension creeping in, they should use the observation to let it go. The leader should ask them to keep their thoughts simple by saying: "Look at those eyes you are seeing and with the simple curiosity of a child, ask yourself, 'Who's in there?'"

The leader might spend a few minutes softly reminding participants to drop their armor more and to slow down as sometimes a group will rush the eye contact. After a while, the leader can rejoin the group.

Gradually, the group will arrive at a very serene and yet powerfully connected place. The participants should try to spend at least three minutes in continual eye contact (more if need be). If it is a large group, the event can go on to 45 minutes.

Generally, the rule is to try to have a good contact with everyone in the group. Naturally, in a large group of ten or more, this isn't practical. If it is allowed to go on too long, the eyes will become fatigued and the mind will become agitated, undoing what has been established.

Break the silence with a few voiced sighs and let everyone stretch a moment and rest the eyes. Afterwards, sit and review the experience.

Angel of Death

This exercise, originally conceived by an influential American Sufi teacher, is simple, but very powerful. It gives the participants a chance to confront their mortality and, as a result, to actualize a profound and wakeful level of personal and theatrical intention. Angel of Death can be played during an improvisation session or as a part of scene work or even as part of a rehearsal for a play. Here's what you do: one person volunteers to be the Angel of Death. This person will enter an improvisation or a scene while it is going on. The actors are to continue undeterred, as if they do not see the Angel. However, whenever the Angel of Death gets in close proximity, the actors must play as if their lives depended upon it. They literally sense death near them and then consciously surrender to the vivid finality of their work, as if experiencing the last moments on earth.

Nobody may exit the scene, but they must instead play fully, allowing the theatrical reality to become absolutely vivid and real to them. Also, the other actors not in direct proximity to the Angel are invited to sense the possible loss of their fellow actor and to play the scene fully, giving their all, wanting the other actor to have the most rewarding and vivid moments of life before the end comes.

The Angel of Death can choose to withdraw, or draw near to the actors, to remain aloof, or if he so chooses, he can touch the actor on the shoulder. The actor, receiving the touch, must allow himself to come to stillness and to reflect keenly and deeply upon his own mortality. As part of that moment, the actor receiving the touch from the Angel must melt down to the floor and surrender to the end. Death has come at last.

This exercise helps to deepen the actors' awareness, gives resonance to any text, and allows the players to raise the stakes to a degree worthy of their desire to live and to live well. Obviously, it is not for the faint of heart, children, or for people who are sentimental about death, but only for those who are mature enough to accept and integrate the powerful realizations that come from such an encounter with mortality.

Obsession

This exercise is uniquely useful for playing farce, satire, clown, and nearly all levels of period and modern comedy. It is designed to liberate the actor into forms of audacious behavior and deft comic choices that have the potential to emerge as great comic invention. It can be used as a teaching tool as well and is very successful as a means to enliven and invigorate the rehearsal process of a show.

Most people take great delight and find much humor in watching their household pets. A pet can be a wonderful resource for comic inspiration. Their antics around the house, their desire to please, and their various unexpected behaviors are often quite hilarious. This is due, in part, to the fact that animals have intentions so direct and pure that they appear to us to be obsessions. Some pets, for example, are obsessed with games, some with treats, some with grooming, and so forth. When an actor adopts a similar purity of intention, she can enter into a wonderful world of comic mayhem.

There are several ways of going about this exercise. In one version, the group is warmed up and ready and the facilitator asks them to mimic one another. My preferred way of doing this is to select one person to stand out of the group near the facilitator while the others enact their versions of that person. For example, if an actor named Susan steps from the group, she would begin to watch a whole room full of "Susans" walking, sitting, and interacting. The members of the group are asked not to satirize their impersonations, but instead to find the essential nature, the core mannerisms and behavioral quirks that are associated with their subject.

From this study, Susan will be able to witness some area of her persona that is at least a little bit obsessive. That obsession will be the starting point for further work in the exercise. Naturally, one by one, all of the other actors will have the opportunity to do the same.

There is another way to begin this exercise and, while not as personally rooted, it has the advantage of getting the exercise started much sooner. In this version, the facilitator prepares a list of obsessions, cuts them up into small leaves of paper, and puts them into a hat or a bag. Then, one by one the actors will reach into the hat and pull out a slip of paper with a word or phrase on it that indicates the form of obsession they will explore in part two of their exercise.

It is helpful to think of obsessions as extensions of what were once called The Seven Deadly Sins: Pride, Avarice, Gluttony, Vanity, Envy, Sloth, and Lust. In this version, Susan might reach into the hat and on her slip of paper might be written: you are obsessed with finding the perfect pair of shoes. Another actor might get one that reads: You have a lust for women's feet. When these two characters interact, we can begin to imagine the comic possibilities.

Once all the participants have their obsessions, the facilitator guides them into a free form exploration of that obsession, letting the actors try out all sorts of behaviors suggested to them by this over-riding behavioral directive. Eventually the actors must be invited to enter into an improvised situation allowing them the chance to pursue their obsessive goals within a specific context. The context can be as simple as having everyone imagine they are attending a tenth year school reunion. It can also be a fun additional element to introduce into the more complicated and structured world of a comic play.

Move 'til You Laugh

This exercise is a great warm-up and a super inhibition breaker. The leader should step out of the work arena for this one to be the ongoing side-coach.

At first, the leader commands the group to move until they genuinely make themselves laugh. The group will inevitably start off way too wild and big and a lot of forced laughter will be heard. After a moment or two, the leader should stop everyone and remind them that the movements need not be huge; in fact, tiny movements may evoke laughter just as well. They should all remember their private moments when they catch themselves doing something absurd or silly. Then with a quick command, they should begin again.

The leader this time just shouts over the din, reminding them to move until they get a genuine laugh. The leader should encourage the group with a few "Yes that's it" and "Go for it, come on!" and any other phrases that boost the group's ability to let go.

There will usually be a peak moment when lots of real laughter is heard. Certainly the movements will be unusual and very hilarious. This is a great exercise to prepare a group for comic characterization and to invoke the light comic spirit they need before a comic performance.

Before long, the laughter will begin to sound wooden again and, at that point, the exercise is over.

Stages of Development

This is an exercise inspired by some of the writings of Philosopher Ken Wilber, especially his book, *Up From Eden*. The ideas presented in his book are based, in part, upon the works of Gene Gebser, Jurgen Habermas, Julian Jaynes, Clare Graves, and many others, most of whom have contributed to what is recently being referred to as "Spiral Dynamics." This model attempts to map the correlations of all previous human cultures within a spectrum of consciousness. In addition to being a cultural map, this spectrum, as Wilber points out, is also represented in our personal development as individuals.

While an entire course of study would be needed to comprehend and apply the principles of Mr. Wilber's thesis, I have constructed the following experience, with a loose and liberal link to his ideas, in order to enhance and strengthen the actor's presence.

It is particularly useful as a means to restore fluidity and wholeness to the psyche and to illustrate the continuum of pure awareness that accompanies all stages of life. A fully integrated psyche weaved together through what might be considered an awareness of awareness keeps the being from getting stuck in one singular stage and allows the actor more transformative possibility.

We begin with the cellular, larval, or archaic stage of life. This is an unthinking and purely subsistence level of being. It is characterized by the simple and primitive drive to survive. In this state we can associate ourselves with the helpless infant, following impulses to secure food, safety, and comfort. Following that we enter the magical stage. Here the infant has grown into a child and at this stage, the movements and events of the unfolding world seem powered by magical forces. Later, the child enters the adolescent stage of the mythical. Here the myths of the past and the present merge as the individual psyche seeks ways to belong to a tribal group, to an identity enlarged by fellows and hero worship. Eventually a rational stage is developed as the individual evolves and appreciates self-determination and the patterns and rational laws of the universe. Beyond this the human being has opportunities to experience the trans-rational stage where the mystical synchronicities and abstract undercurrents are experienced on a higher level. Finally, the human being advances to the transpersonal stage, a level of development that transcends and yet includes all the other levels.

It is necessary to have a facilitator to guide this exercise. Each participant starts out laying on his back, preferably on a mat surface, but any clean open floor space will do. After the group is situated, focused, and in position with arms relaxed at the sides, the facilitator begins with the following:

Take three deep breaths. On the last exhale allow your body to relax completely. Next, empty your mind of all chatter and extraneous thoughts. In fact, remove all cognitive activity and simply find contentment in just being there. Relish simple presence. Next, imagine you are a single cell, just a single amorphous shape. Begin to move the body as a simple single cell. Allow this cell to have the desire to explore, to move and expand. Do this for at least ten minutes.

Next, expand your growth to become a larva, a faceless shape with just the tiniest glimmer of self-awareness. Give over to any and all movements and sounds suggested by becoming this larva. Allow yourself the luxury of following just the simple and natural impetus to move in any direction. In this stage, you need not be as amorphous as the single cell. Here you will adopt a focal point such as a knee, or buttocks, or a hand to become the head, guiding the larval movements in one direction or another.

After five or ten minutes of this, progress to the infancy stage. Begin lying on your back on the mat and sense the room around you. Gradually begin to breathe younger and younger until your breath approximates the soft unobstructed breath of an infant. Eventually begin to crawl and coo and explore with the natural curiosity of a baby, making sounds and relating to the other babies if the moment arises. Be careful not to force moments or to imitate. Live each and every moment as the infant moving your obviously overlarge body with easy and open curiosity. (Allow at least ten minutes or more.) Some babies will become fascinated by color, some by sounds, some by the movement of other babies, some by their own toes, and so forth. Simply follow the natural flow of curiosity, letting each moment unfold in whatever form it must. Above all, avoid the temptation to make something interesting happen. Stay absolutely committed to the simplicity of deep moment-to-moment discovery.

Now progress to become a toddler. At this stage, you can speak some words and have more interest in social interaction. You are experimenting with walking, toddling along from place to place, occasionally finding yourself sitting on the mat with a little "kaboom." Use your limited language ability to extend your sense of self, responding naturally and without the need to force anything interesting to occur. (Allow ten to fifteen minutes.)

This progression can scale up the age ladder, re-experiencing each of the aptitudes and developmental stages of childhood. It is best to select grade levels as well as ages since some participants have difficulty placing themselves at six years old, but they can easily put themselves in first grade. I also suggest moving in two- or three-year units of time. The differences between being eight and then nine years old, while profound to us at the time, are very difficult to re-examine and re-experience in an exercise format. However, if time permits and the inclination is to delve more fully into the re-capturing of those discrete years, the facilitator can guide the group year by year. Or, if time is limited, the group can agree ahead of time to leap over a few stages, perhaps starting up again in early adolescence.

In that scenario, the facilitator would continue guiding the exercise, creating scenarios for easy interaction at each stage of development.

If at twelve or thirteen years of age, it is fun for the participants to begin to relate to each other as if in school during a recess. Give yourself plenty of opportunity to express your thoughts, your ideas, to question the authorities, parents, and the experts. Notice the inclination to gather in gender groups and to discuss the world with one another in teams. Notice the interest in pop stars, athletes, and all manner of iconic figures.

Now progress to late teens where the concerns are almost all part of the mating ritual. Notice how the earlier dependence upon groups and teams now gives way to more individuality and independence. Notice the inclination towards invincibility and the pressures to define one's career path.

Move on to mid-twenties and the early advent of career pursuits. Here the concerns are more firmly rooted in establishing a foothold in the society, in a career identity, the start of a family, and the individual quest for achievement within a cultural context. It is good to enhance this portion of the exercise with some sort of context. Perhaps the participants are at a reunion, a block party, a political gathering, or a conference. Create a situation whereby those fully invested in the exercise can willingly and effortlessly enter into it and begin to speak and relate as if the context were really happening. If the reason to gather is not convincing, this part of the exercise will dissolve quickly.

Give the group about ten minutes or so to begin to establish relationships and to begin to formulate agendas and behavioral identities.

Up until this point, the human being as experienced in the exercise, moves through stages of growth associated with an age level. The first stage is considered to be larval or archaic. It is the natural precognitive cellular expression of the body. Here the primal instincts are all that matters. There is no morality, no belief system, just simple but very powerful instinctual needs. The next stage of the infant and child is considered to be magical. The child infers certain abilities and magical powers from the world, sees the interplay of forces and the uniquely fresh unfolding of events and formulates an imaginative interplay with them.

As the child evolves and enters the next level of development, the personal magical universe of the infant and young child gives way gradually to the mythical/tribal stage. The child comes to realize that he or she does not have certain powers. Therefore, the forces of the universe must derive from larger, more powerful figures. It is at this stage that hero-worship and mythically-devised role models become paramount.

The next stage involves the introduction of personal responsibility and a rational explanation of the world. This rational perspective, once instilled and supported by a social structure at or around the same stage usually becomes the dominant perspective throughout the life span of most people living in developed societies. The blossoming of the rational scientific point of view is prime example. Most people in the developed world are profoundly steeped in a rational understanding of their world and only in a few areas of our lives do we permit non-rational ideas to exist. We no longer associate the shifts of fortune in our lives to the whims of external gods, goddesses, or celestial alignments. Instead, our society teaches us to see the heavens as a solar system in a galaxy of other solar systems and our earthly life as an outgrowth of organic, social, and economic processes.

The stages of life experienced in the exercise are not mathematical equations of immutable laws. They do not represent categories that are sharply delineated. The complex and conglomerate human psyche is much more fully integrated than that and the sense memory recall is holistic. Nevertheless, they do provide a convenient way to look at our development and to find more ownership of the whole being, which in turn inspires similar ownership in a solid fictional characterization.

Most modern societies support the growth arc through the developmental stages, culminating at the rational stage. The consensus view of reality does not yet recognize the existence of higher stages of development. Therefore, the next levels of development are not automatic and are achieved only after a great amount of concerted effort. Whenever the social structure of a nation or group of nations remains stuck at a particular level, any attempt to transcend and go beyond it will feel and certainly look like someone foolishly swimming upstream against the prevailing current. It falls to those groups and pioneers on the fringe edges of the mainstream societies to investigate and progress beyond the consensus level. It takes extraordinary energy to evolve beyond the dominant center of gravity of one's society, but it can be done. Mavericks and various secret groups have succeeded throughout history as have the rare nation state such as pre-invasion Tibet.

The middle age experience should produce a trans-rational perspective whereby the vicissitudes of life and the dreamlike patterns of synchronicity merge to provide a point of view rich with symbol, metaphor, instinctual wisdom, and irony. In old age, there is another level to be reached, sometimes referred to as "transpersonal." This is the level that includes and incorporates all of the lower levels in a perspective that transcends personal ego. Transpersonal levels are characterized by great tolerance, humor, a wisdom that includes dream states, rational scientific regard, mystical merging, and timeless cosmological insight.

Often the stories enacted in plays and movies represent the struggle of a person or group in their effort to rise above their level of awareness. These are usually sociological evolutions being depicted through personal epiphanies and growth spurts brought on through the dynamic encounter or conflict of one kind or another. They describe how the protagonists' new understanding blends the lower levels into a new rationality or, increasingly, a new trans-rational and even transpersonal perspective. Today's world is now chock-a-block with programs and plays that deal with issues and ideas that are clearly reaching beyond the rational ceiling implied by society at large.

We must, as philosopher Ken Wilber suggests, "transcend and include" all lower levels if we are to progress without pathologies. This exercise helps to bring the participant up to the rational level of awareness in preparation for transcendence and inclusion. Experiencing these stages of awareness as stages of our human chronological journey helps the participant to see it as a natural phenomenon. The astonishing thing is to realize that not only do individual people travel through these stages, but entire civilizations and, indeed, the entire arc of human history is moving through these stages. Will we, as a species, manage to grow up and make it to the transpersonal stage?

Friends or Family Member

This exercise is loads of fun and allows participants to immerse themselves into a characterization that they often find to be surprisingly, perhaps even shockingly transformative. Here's what to do. Giving at least a two-week preparation time in advance, have all the actors in the group prepare to come to the workspace at a specific time. At the assigned time they will arrive as a close friend or family member and they are to remain in character throughout the preset time period.

This is a superb exercise to integrate with costume and makeup courses since the expectation is that the actor will arrive completely disguised and transformed. By keeping the character choice close to home the actor has more access to the psychology and the behavioral nuances of the character, yet the ideal scenario is that the actor is convincingly transformed.

The facilitator will need to create a context for all of these different people to come together. It could be a sales seminar, a hospital waiting room, a holding room during a flight delay, and so on. Obviously, the facilitator must remain in character as the seminar leader or host, providing information and activities that get these people to interact with one another.

Once the characters arrive and begin to mingle and improvise within the given circumstances, the facilitator needs only to step out of the way and let the events naturally unfold.

Time Traveling

This is one of a number of "threshold exercises" I have used to help actors access their will center. It is very demanding and should be done with the utmost seriousness and care.

This one does require music. I often use slow, melodic harp music to give the room a gentle ambiance. Participants should be dressed comfortably, a sweat suit or dance attire is ideal. No jewelry or junk in pockets. I suggest bare feet as well.

The leader does *not* participate in this event. In fact, it is useful to have an assistant, especially if it is a large group (10 or more).

The event should happen in a secure spacious room, preferably on a wood floor. Concrete or carpeted surfaces are difficult for this work and should be avoided if at all possible. The room should be a comfortable temperature with proper ventilation.

To begin, following a short warm-up, everyone will lie down on the floor on his or her back, leaving ample room around them. Keep the music going throughout. And remind the group that they should go to the restroom before they begin. There's nothing more frustrating than doing this exercise with a throbbing bladder. Then, the leader should lead the group through a few deep breaths, to settle the system and focus the mind.

Although directions were explained beforehand, the leader should once again reiterate what they are about to do: they are asked to go from their prone position to a standing position in a slow and continuous manner. The slow is extremely slow—the slowest they have ever moved! It should take two hours to stand completely.

It is important to remind the group that their movements are to be continuous, flowing, and slow. Even their eyes, tongue, and facial movements should be very slow.

If it happens, and it often does, that they find themselves in a bind, they must solve the problem with the same slow movement.

To make it easier, I have on occasion demonstrated a simple trajectory that will save them a lot of steps. From the prone position, I first roll my head to one side, then my opposite arm comes across my chest and my opposite knee lifts and crosses, effectively putting me on one side. I then struggle to free the arm under me. Next, I maneuver myself to all fours, separate my feet and slowly rock back into a squat position. From here, and with my head hanging, I lift the hips, straightening the legs, and eventually roll up the spine.

Everyone is different. Each will inevitably find personal variations on that trajectory, but it will at least provide a pattern to follow if they get in a super bind. Speaking of binds, once in a while someone will get the body into a real doosie of a position and because of the placement—a shirt is obstructing the mouth, or whatever—he or she may need assistance. The leader and the assistant should keep watch for such situations and offer only the minimum necessary help to get the person back on track again. Keep in mind, there is much to be learned by the obstacles encountered on this slow journey, so don't feel obliged to save them from the work challenges.

Although grueling at times, the exercise is also filled with amazing and very useful rewards. For one, the participants come face to face with their little angel that says, "Aw, go ahead, you can cheat a little here—no one will notice"; and even more importantly, they come face to face with the will center which demands accuracy and honest work effort.

There is a psychic level to the event as well. The slow movement seems to put the mind into orbit. Memories, dreams, voices, and all manner of mental phenomena start to unfold, creating additional struggle for the participant, working to maintain an intention to stand at the same slow, continuous pace. It helps if the leader says slowly and softly some of the following phrases every ten minutes or so:

"Resist the temptation to go fast."

"Stay slow, you have all the time in the world."

"Keep your focus here in the room –
going from this position to a stand."

"If you get in a bind, reverse at the same slow pace
and try another solution."

"Don't forget to breathe."

Before beginning, make sure none of the participants are dealing with an injury or illness. Diabetics, or even borderline diabetics, should not do this exercise.

The leader is also the timekeeper and should tell the group when they are 1/4 finished, 1/2, 3/4, and then nearing the two-hour mark. Of course, everyone does not have to finish at two hours. Some will finish earlier, some later. Impress upon the group, however, that they should make it at least to the 3/4 mark.

When they come to a stand and as the head lifts, the leader or assistant should whisper to them to take a few steps and then gradually find a chair and sit down. The assistant should have ready some cups of water for everyone and some tissue for those who are releasing emotionally. There are occasions when a participant needs a tissue during the work, and I have, as the leader, simply held the tissue to the nose and done the honors without too much fuss.

The effects of the time-traveling event vary widely. Some participants burst into tears, others feel a deep peace, others feel powerful—like they could run a marathon—and some are just plain exhausted. All of them, however, have a new awareness of themselves and a renewed confidence in their abilities.

They will also, no doubt, have experienced time as an elastic or liquid concept, no longer exerting a rigid stranglehold on their awareness. By experiencing this new stage of being (and it is definitely an altered state), the participants are given a new reference point for their sense of time. Changing their relationship to time can endow them with new possibilities and the will to accomplish their highest ideals.

This event should not be done more than once in any three-day period. As an added challenge, the time-travel should be longer if only by five minutes, each time it is done. This is very demanding work, so it must be treated with the utmost care and respect.

Taking a Stand

This exercise can be loads of fun and ignites the creative and passionate fires within. It also firmly establishes the importance of personalizing one's work and of having a well-defined point of view. The inspiration for this exercise came from a moment when I witnessed Tibetan monks performing a form of sporting high-powered cosmic debate. These debates are a part of a monk's training regimen and can be wildly passionate, fast paced, and obviously very challenging. They argue their views with the force, power, vitality, and stamina resembling an Olympic athlete in full stride.

Think about it. How often do you get the chance to stand up for what you know and to engage in a full-out verbal sparring match purely for the fun of it? There are two ways to approach this exercise and both have enormous value. The first way is to enter into the game as oneself, taking a hot topic or a personally held point of view and then stepping forth to declare it. In this version, the exercise is a dynamic forum whereby you go on record and are willing to take a stand to defend and to convince others of your point of view. The second way is doing the exact same thing only in this version, you are the advocate for a character in a play, preferably a character you have played or are about to play in a scene or production. You can be the character if you feel that to be more valuable, or you can be yourself in the role of professional advocate for your character's point of view.

Here's what happens: the person taking a stand literally stands up and faces a panel of four other seated participants whose function it is to argue the opposing view or to call the person on weak logic or poor commitment; in other words, the devil's advocate position. The various challenges from the panel are all designed to stimulate the individual person or character advocate into formulating a clear, coherent, consistent, and convincing foundation for the chosen point of view.

The authority and clarity gained from this is enormously valuable. For one thing, it exercises a muscle that goes relatively unused in modern polite societies and it brings to light all sorts of useless flotsam and jetsam that may be in the way of effective communication. It can reveal certain body language problems, vocal problems, speech habits, energy problems, and credibility weaknesses that might be halting the true flow of intention from the speaker. It will also bring to light the effective and truly convincing qualities of the speaker.

When linked to a character in a play, the exercise fleshes out the character's persona, gives depth and breadth to the imagined circumstances, and helps the actor discover the heart and soul of the character's filter on the world, allowing more effective communion with the other actors and characters within the given circumstances.

Special Advice: This may bring up many personal issues, reveal vulnerabilities, and expose areas of the shadow side of all participants.

It is important to acknowledge them, but not particularly useful to indulge them. In other words, it is the energy and solidity and courage gained from the exercise that is of real value. The personal knots and stories associated with whatever arises are only a distraction and can often take the exercise off track or worse, give the participants a rationale for avoiding going on record. It is also important to mention that everyone needs to accept that all points of view are valuable, that people change their points of view, and that we, as whole human beings, are not reducible to any one point of view. It is only the filter we have devised to cope with the world and to derive meaning and safety. Finally, if the exercise collapses under too much emotional weight or gets out of control, the group as a whole, under the guidance of the facilitator, are advised to sit and chant the mantra, Zen za Hu Ma, for at least fifteen minutes or until someone gets one.

Mocumentary

I have done this exercise several times and it never fails to launch the participants into a multi-dimensional play space that opens up moments, atmospheres, and entire scenes of extraordinary richness. What is truly amazing about this exercise is that everyone, regardless of their level of experience, will be swept up into the agreed-upon reality and will inevitably have moments of surprising greatness.

Here's what you do. As a group, create a fictional premise that allows all of the characters to interact. It could be as simple as creating a diner in a small town where people come and go as part of their everyday lives. It could be a group of law students struggling to prepare for and pass the bar exam. It could be a fledgling protest group preparing for their big protest day. Whatever it is, it needs to be an idea that is convincing enough to justify the coming together of the various types of people in the group and engaging enough to allow people to commit to vivid imaginative play.

Once the idea is agreed upon and everyone has a basic idea of the premise, then the group must settle upon the possible characters that inhabit this world. The characters need all to have histories, strong needs, relationships, and a secret inner life. The characters must be real enough to belong convincingly to the world they will inhabit, but they must have traits that are magnified just enough to have a slightly satiric sheen to them.

Next, a small film crew needs to be assembled. The ideal scenario is that the facilitator or teacher gets the camera, has editing access, and can commit the time and energy needed to complete the project.

This exercise will only work if everyone commits to a few basic laws.

First, when the camera is rolling, everyone stays in character, regardless of what happens. Second, everyone should stay on task with the character's needs, but share the scene with others. Third, set a very strict shooting schedule and stick to it no matter what.

The actors will soon come to realize the magic of having a "recording consciousness" in the room with them. The pact to remain in character solidifies the secondary reality so acutely that it quickly becomes the primary reality, getting more and more vivid, seeming more and more "real." In the end, all participants come away with a renewed faith in their ability to go with the flow, a deeper respect for the shifting of realities, and hopefully a fun and funny record of the magical moments caught by the camera.

Playing an Action

Effectively define and play an action is the basis for all good acting. It is the very foundation upon which any skilled actor, regardless of the circumstances, must build. It harkens back to the earlier chapter "The Antidote to Narcissism," and like most things, it is much easier to talk about and conceptualize than actually to do. That is why some teachers have chosen to alter the vocabulary from "play your action" to "do your doings." Hopefully, after some experience with this exercise you will have a REAL taste of what it is to play an action.

To begin, let's answer the question: What is an action? An action is a behavioral event that seeks to affect the behavior and/or point of view of one or more other characters within the world of the play or film. It is guided by intention, context, and character point of view. When arranged in a clear sentence form, it becomes a definition that stimulates emotional freedom and imaginative play between actors. A good action propels the actor into living truthfully by having a clear, secure, and do-able task. It must be in alignment with the needs of the character, appropriate to the play and the production, simple and direct, and above all, linked toward outcomes that affect others. It is most effective when an actor manages to personalize it by finding links to his or her own life experience.

Most modern acting texts have references to actions. They all supply in some form or another a definition and reference to what it is to play an action. Few of them, however, really admit to the fact that it is necessary and takes a considerable amount of work to dislodge the usual social buffers we all employ. Then, in addition, it takes more time to allow the emotional instrument to begin to function with free and open reflexes that express themselves with the right measure of truth and in ways unique to the individual. Even if an actor is a genius at defining an action, if his instrument hasn't been allowed the laboratory time to practice the uninhibited response reflex and to work out the kinks, he will do nothing but act a "concept" of the action. This is the most common malady afflicting beginning actors.

In order to play an action it is important to have it clearly defined in a manner that is potent emotionally, engages the other actor, and can be played with real personal investment. However, the ultimate effectiveness of the action will depend upon the actor's level of experience and the accuracy of his behavioral reflexes. There are several levels of sophistication in playing an action as well. If you want television soap operas, for example, much of the style of acting depends upon playing large, relatively obvious actions, behaviors that seemingly obscure the underlying intention from the character but reveal it to the camera. This is commonly called "indicating" and is the least sophisticated form of acting.

Actors in more demanding styles of acting are careful *not* to indicate their intention, but instead maintain a strong need to affect the other person in ways that are appropriate to the play and truly aim to stimulate the reflexes and imagination of the fellow player.

Shakespearean actors often fall into the poetry trap of the classical plays, playing the audience's point of view of the character as if they were obligated to show how evil the evil guy is or how virtuous the Queen is, and so forth. When the actor moves beyond that and begins to see through the point of view of the character and what the character's needs are and what he or she is hoping to effect in the others in this fictional world, the acting becomes quite human, seemingly very immediate, and fun to watch.

To sense character point of view as opposed to the audience point of view, imagine that Richard the Third knows he is being bad, but he also knows that he is having great fun, and he truly believes that his charms, his wit and strategic use of power, will make him a rock star in the eyes of the others. He honestly believes that by unleashing the full power of his devious mind, he will save the land from ruin and establish the kind of new order that will be exciting to explore and a wonder to behold. He isn't jumping around acting evil; instead he simply shuns all such silly labels and pursues his goals with all the gusto he can muster, believing that the ends justify the means. Richard the Second, often played like a whining sap, is not a forlorn romantic who loves to wax poetic. He is an immature king who honestly believes that by using poetic imagery and constant reminders of his divine rights he can inspire those around him just to stop their savage intrigues and halt the progress of the impending coup. He thinks that he can stimulate the childlike wonder in others and alter their judgments of him by his unique use of language and the display of his own childlike trust in his divinity.

Once character point of view is established the action needs to be defined. Staying within the world of Shakespeare for the moment, let us look at a role that is by its very nature somewhat resistant to action: Oberon from *A Midsummer Night's Dream*. Oberon has several long passages of verse where he recounts in elaborate detail certain past events. It is tempting simply to say that he is King of the woodland Faeries and that is the way he talks. However, that reasoning is passive and will result in a speechy interpretation, slowing the momentum of the play while this particular character does a "poetry solo." Why does Oberon go on and on? What could possibly be the action that justifies his elaborations?

Let's look at the following unit of dialogue from *A Midsummer Night's Dream*:

Oberon:
My gentle puck, come hither. Thou rememberest
Since once I sat upon a promontory
And heard a mermaid on a dolphin's back
Uttering such dulcet and harmonious breath
That the rude sea grew civil at her song
And certain stars shot madly from their spheres
To hear the sea maid's music?

Robin:
I remember

Oberon:
That very time I saw, but thou could'st not,
Flying between the cold moon and the earth
Cupid, all armed. A certain aim he took
At a fair vestal throned by the west,
And loosed his love-shaft smartly from his bow
As it should pierce a hundred thousand hearts.
But I might see young Cupid's fiery shaft
Quenched in the chaste beams of the wat'ry moon,
And the imperial vot'ress passed on,
In maiden meditation, fancy-free
Yet marked I where the bolt of Cupid fell.
It fell upon a little western flower—
Before, milk-white; now, purple with love's wound:
And maidens call it 'love in idleness'.
Fetch me this flower; the herb I showed thee once.
The juice of it on sleeping eyelids laid
Will make a man or woman madly dote
Upon the next living creature that it sees.
Fetch me this herb, and be thou here again
Ere the leviathan can swim a league.

Robin:
I'll put a girdle round the earth in forty minutes. Exit.[1]

It is tempting to assume that Oberon is just a wordy guy who loves to paint verbal pictures. Or that this is Shakespeare's wink toward the royals as he recounts the time Queen Elizabeth was treated to a massive celebration at Kenilworth castle, complete with a mechanical dolphin, a singer in a mermaid costume, and a proposal of marriage from the Earl of Leister (which she steadfastly refused). Yet, consider that the end of his speech to Robin is an admonition to do his work in haste. If we choose to remain true to the world of the play, we must ask: if Oberon is in such a hurry, why is he wasting so much time talking?

Or more specifically, for what does Oberon wax poetic? The answer to that question moves the actor forward into a definition of an action that is in keeping with the text and allows for a more engaged approach to the moments on stage.

Oberon calls his woodland helper, "gentle" Puck, and then begins his speech to him by recounting a memory that clearly he knows Puck will recall. However, he reveals an aspect of the memory that Puck never before heard, an element of the event that had until now remained secret. What does an actor do with this text? How can the actor make sense of all this storytelling at such an urgent time?

It seems to me that Oberon must win Robin over. Perhaps Puck (Puck is Robin's nickname) is frightened by the argument between Oberon and Titania that transpired moments before and Oberon must reassure him, must calm him, must perhaps lure him out of hiding. Perhaps Puck is in awe of celestial gods like Cupid and Oberon is entertaining him a bit, by giving him a blow-by-blow account of the event, perhaps as a way of helping him forget his fear and get focused for the task ahead. In this way the descriptive elements serve to invite Puck forward, serve to adjust his mood, and bring him forth.

Puck's reward for coming out of hiding is that he is let into Oberon's secret. Perhaps Puck aspires to become a wizard-like presence in the forest, and Oberon, knowing this, guarantees Puck's loyalty and speed by allowing Puck, for the first time, to acquire some very real and very special forest magic.

Or we could go another direction: perhaps Puck is thick-headed and needs lots of description to really "get it." In this approach, Puck would need careful storytelling so that he fully understood. Or perhaps Puck is a vain and somewhat haughty creature; one who hates to run errands. In this scenario, Oberon must craft the story so vividly that the idea of what to do emerges in Puck's mind, and in spite of his pre-disposition, he becomes charged with the energy to do Oberon's bidding.

There are countless other possibilities. The point being that even in a scene like this where there are classical language challenges, it is imperative for the actor to define clearly the "action." Once this is defined, the actor is free to play, living moment to moment, reacting to all the behavioral cues from his fellow actor. The actor playing Oberon can now use all of his language and delivery skills to achieve his goal with Puck. In this way he will avoid the usual pomposities associated

with large Shakespearean speeches and the play will have real momentum.

A well-defined action is aimed toward the other character or characters. The aim is to ignite something within them, to inspire them, to
change their point of view in order to fulfill a need. If Oberon truly
needs Robin to dash off and retrieve this special herb, he must speak to
him in a way that will accomplish this. Keep in mind that characters
do not plan to do a monologue. They only continue speaking because,
obviously, their first attempts have not done the trick; have not accomplished their action.

Here's what to do: have the group break up into two-person teams.
They should be handed a short script that has a somewhat balanced
split of lines. In other words, it is not fair to have one character who is
speaking in long monologues while the other says only one or two
lines. The teams are quickly to memorize a ten-line unit of the scene
and then begin to define for themselves what their respective actions
might be. It is not necessary for the partners to share everything about
their definition. Some of the more potent elements need to remain as
personal secrets.

After working on the first unit of the scenes, present them for the
group. Is the definition of each action potent enough to inspire the
imagination? Is the action engaging enough to draw the actor into the
scene, into playing with his or her partner without self-consciousness
or the need to entertain the viewer? Are the actors invested fully and
is there a strong need driving the action? Is this action appropriate for
the scene?

Now, one of the common pitfalls in this process is creating a definition of an action that is inner instead of outer directed. Often, an
actor will choose to define his action in terms of his own emotional
state. He may say that his goal is to show the other character how upset
he is or how much pain he feels. While this may be a common device
in life, it is ineffective in the acting craft. Instead, that actor needs to
re-define the action as an outer directed impulse. In this manner he
may state his goal is to inspire compassion in the other person, to shock
her into having an epiphany, to lure her into having an emotional experience, to seduce her into confessing her heart's desire. In this way of
thinking, each participant is busy listening and responding to the other
person in a manner conducive to real communion. When this height-

ened level of awareness is clicking, there is nothing quite like it. It is a form of human interaction that is uniquely pleasurable both to experience and to witness.

When the first ten lines or so are starting to emerge with truth and with focused actions, the teams should take on more and more of the scene until they have memorized it in its entirety. At this stage the questions to ask are: Does the initial action sustain throughout the scene? Do I need to raise the stakes? What is my character's ideal outcome in this scene? What are the obstacles to my character's goal? Am I open and available, truly listening to my partner, or am I too wrapped up in my own world to react truthfully?

Spend some time answering these questions, and then rehearse the scene over and over again, seeking to dispel any extraneous brain chatter, negative message loops, or judgments.

The repetition will help to eliminate the pedestrian noise in the consciousness and if each actor stays true to his or her well-defined action, they should lift off into a transcendent state together.

One last pitfall to address: playing the problem. It is often the case that characters are in highly stressful or emotionally dynamic situations. The character has a problem on one or more levels and the script may even describe or reveal the problem in the dialogue. Inexperienced actors will "play" that problem as if they needed to demonstrate it for the other character or to enact the implied emotional state. However, it is infinitely more viable and truthful to have the problem but to play the action. In other words, even if a character says that he is at the end of his rope and actually feels terribly desperate, the actor must play the action, must play the intention of revealing this desperation. The character has a problem, but he is speaking to the other character in order to accomplish what? Remember, don't ask why a character says something, ask "What for?"

When an actor learns to define an action in terms of affecting the other on stage, remains available and open to the other actor's action, and avoids playing the problem, the foundation of a heightened reality emerges and the players will at last be playing truthfully within imaginary circumstances.

The Messiah

There is a teaching in the Kabbalah (the mystical Hebrew tradi-

tion), originally introduced by Rabbi Isaac Luria in the sixteenth century, that perceives the concept of the Messiah not as the coming of a
person, but as a symbol of world harmony.

Legend has it that Luria gathered his disciples one Sabbath. He
made it clear that there must be complete harmony among them all
throughout the duration of the Sabbath. They were not even to have the
slightest confrontation. This they did until near the end; a trivial argument broke out which escalated to a disagreement between two disciples. He later explained to them that because of their weaknesses,
Satan had worked again to create disunity and forestall the Messiah.

The following exercise uses this premise to create an improvisational situation that can help activate new levels of characterization.
This exercise is a variation on the Hebraic theme except the characters
gathered are not disciples but total strangers. Inherent in this fact is a
certain tension and distance between the various types of people. Their
task then is to establish some form of complete harmony.

What happens is this: each person in the group arrives "in character." How the characters are developed is up to the class. (In my classes, this exercise is used after the students have completed at least three
weeks of character research and development.) They should know
their characters well enough to remain in character, respond and react
in character, and immerse themselves in the scenario in character for at
least an hour.

Once all the characters have arrived, the leader welcomes everyone and, in a pleasant manner, tells them the following: "I know you
are all anxious to discover exactly what you are doing here and how
you came to be here with everyone else. That will all become clear as
we progress. Let me first say there is no need to panic, all your needs
in terms of food, air, and water will be taken care of. My superiors
have instructed me not to tell you anything else at this time other than
that you are asked to meet one another and get to know each other
before my next visit.

"There is no need to try to escape through the door(s) or window (s)
because what you perceive as solid matter is, in fact, nothing more than
a hologram supported by your collective thought patterns. And please
do not be alarmed by my sudden appearance or disappearance; this is a
natural function that will also become clear to you in the near future.
Until then, I bid you goodbye."

I usually snap my fingers, as if I had disappeared, and then I can step "unseen" to a chair along one of the walls to sit and observe.

A number of things might happen at this point, and obviously, much depends on the characters assembled. Whatever happens, it is important that no one look at the leader or allow in any way his or her invisible presence to invade their reality. Early interactions may be slow and possibly confused at first. Inevitably, the first attempts at character improv will sound terribly trite and just plain phony. As they progress, however, this aspect improves immensely.

Characters who are natural leaders might start the ball rolling by introducing themselves to people or making a speech or investigating the room, looking for a way out. The leader should just sit by and let things take their course. After about ten minutes, the leader should snap back in and provide the next instructions. Do not be surprised if characters talk to you and want to know more than you are telling them; evade their questions as well as you can. The next instructions go something like this: "Hello again, I hope you all had enough time to acquaint yourselves with one another. My superiors have told me to inform you of your situation. Some of you come from different times and different backgrounds. The reason you all can meet here is that this is a holding chamber between realities. You are neither alive, as you once were, nor are you dead. You are at an in-between place that has no time.

"You must decide among yourselves if you want to stay here together for eternity, or return to your former lives. To return, however, takes a special effort on everyone's part. In order to dissolve the hologram, everyone here must decide upon and enact a group ritual of complete harmony lasting for at least one minute. When this is done, you will return instantly."

It never fails that there follows a burst of questions or reactions, even during the speech, so the leader should remain flexible. If a question pops up that cannot be fielded, the leader can always say he will ask his superior and then snap out of the scene to plan the next tactic.

This is when things start to heat up. Some characters are thrust into despair, others seem indifferent, some even think it's an elaborate joke. Gradually, the characters struggle to arrive at a plan of action. Of course, human nature makes it difficult for people to agree on anything, and this common attribute is usually heightened by people in character.

This stage can go free-flow anywhere between ten and twenty minutes, at which time, the next instruction is given: "I am sorry to have to tell you this, but there has been a change of instruction. You no longer have the option to stay here together for eternity. If you do not complete a unified ritual within the next ten minutes, you will be taken from here and killed one by one. If in ten minutes you are unable to unify, then you must decide on who will be the first sacrifice. That is all I can tell you for now. Good luck."

Now this is a little cheesy, I know, but it serves to intensify the experience. The time limit zooms everyone to action and yields some very interesting results. It is especially interesting to see how they go about finding a ritual. Or, if a ritual is not found, it is equally interesting to see how they go about selecting the first sacrifice.

At exactly ten minutes, the leader should re-enter and demand to be given the sacrifice. Unless, of course, they have unified, in which case the exercise comes to a halt and the actors can drop character and discuss the discoveries.

If a sacrifice is taken, the leader and the person will snap out and watch the next sequence of events together from the sidelines. Several sacrifices can be taken or sometimes it is useful to send back the first one who relates a story of unspeakable torture and horror and tries to convince them of the importance of enacting the ritual.

If it appears that there will never be the ritual, the leader should end the improvisation and allow everyone to discuss the event.

The rituals themselves can be just about anything. That is part of the charm of the exercise. It's fun to see what a particular group will use to display their attempts to unify. I have done many of these exercises and only twice have I witnessed a truly unified ritual. Both times it was a struggle, but a glorious thing to see when it happened.

It may take a few of these impovs to bring the characters to full shape. The dangers involved are the characters making their moments too melodramatic or the opposite, undervaluing their situation. Occasionally, I have interrupted the exercise and challenged the group to place themselves more fully in the situation, as if it were real.

Of course, as in all such exercises, participants are not allowed to abuse, physically, anyone else or in any way to threaten the safety of the participants. I will allow things to heat up, but if it starts to build to physical violence I yell, "freeze!" reminding them of their task to ride the edge of the reality, but not to fall into it.

Filters

I love this exercise. It combines the best of the newer acting technologies with the added advantage of exposing the psychological mechanism that has produced so much suffering. The beauty of it is the utter simplicity of the experience. This exercise, more than any other, if done correctly, can last a lifetime and can make any actor's job infinitely easier.

While good acting is all about unique behavioral specifics, characters can be described in general terms. Those descriptions, however, are the conclusions that are drawn from the perspective of the reader or the viewer. If a character is viewed as an arrogant character, for example, an inexperienced actor will often choose to portray the overall quality of arrogance. What results is a hackneyed and cliché version of "arrogance." Remember, however, that the actor must live only the character's perspective.

Now here's the fun part. Consider how the colorized gel filter placed in front of a theatrical spotlight works. Flip the frame and a new color arrives. A similar filter system is in place in the human psyche in a very unique and interesting way. So the actor playing the arrogant character must, instead of acting arrogant, put in the "arrogant filter." What this means is that an arrogant character doesn't walk around acting arrogant, instead, he simply sees the world as not worth his trouble and time. With this filter in place, anything the actor sees or hears or feels is experienced as beneath him. The other actors, the furniture, the props, virtually everything around the actor is there as reinforcement of character. Suddenly the actor is free to play and be spontaneous instead of forcing himself to portray character qualities.

The facilitator guides the group into adopting a number of filters. When asked to put in a filter, they are free to speak or not to speak, to move around the room, sit, or interact at will.

It is best to begin with bold filters. Start with arrogance and let everyone play with that filter for a while. After experiencing this filter for some time, the facilitator guides them in the following manner:

Come back to neutral. Now let's go the opposite direction. Lets put in the filter of "humility." A truly humble person doesn't walk around acting humble. Instead, he simply sees the world and the people around him as awesome, beautiful, and truly extraordinary. See the space and these people, and select specific things as data to support your point of view. In other words, don't act! Simply get the evidence that is all around you.

The facilitator can now guide the group to experience the filters of paranoia, then unconditional love, compassion, then cruelty, or any and all inventions truly playable by the actors. Of course, in the end, characters are complex, three-dimensional beings that cannot be reduced to a single quality. However, by experiencing the filters exercise, the actor can begin to know how effortless characterization can be. More importantly, he or she can have the realization that we are responsible for our perceptions.

We all have conditioned reflex filters that are in place and this exercise makes it possible to see how we may be liberated from this conditioning, so choose setting the stage for real growth and evolution.

Life Review

This is a private exercise that can be done anytime anywhere. All that is needed is a sincere effort to maintain a certain perspective for a specific span of time. It is a very transformative exercise when done fully and because of that, the "player" should avoid diffusing its power by talking about it.

The exercise is this: at a predetermined time of day, the player decides to alter his perspective of reality for a full hour—with no lapses. He or she, during that hour, observes and participates in life as if he or she were experiencing the *life review* which occurs at the moment of death. One believes one is dead and, at the same time, part of the consciousness knows it is living.

There can be poignancy as each moment unfolds. The exercise is different for everyone and a lot depends on where one is and what one is doing. What seems universal is a sense of wanting to be the kind of person and do the kinds of things that will not make the review seem banal. Everyone reports a deepening of values and a renewed appreciation for moment–to–moment existence.

When people practice this exercise regularly over a period of time, they can begin to live their lives differently. Their work as actors improves immensely, and they begin to want to take their growth seriously. Most of all, there seems to be more love and forgiveness generated.

While not directly applicable to the stage, this exercise, in an indirect way, is working the muscles of observation and of the special concentration needed to maintain character perspective. Plus, with the added incentive to do quality work, there is often marked improvement on all levels of the actor's craft.

I mentioned earlier not to talk away the energy of this exercise. By that I mean to say, avoid telling anyone what is going on during the work hour. There can be some minimal discussion in the group to clarify things and to let people validate their experiences, but for the most part, it is much more effective when done privately.

Metaphysics

Although I prefer to limit acting techniques to the studio and the professional arena, there are a few simple, subtle, and useful exercises that actors can do in ordinary life that can contribute to their overall development. These are small conscious efforts that boost the actor's energy, focus, and self-confidence.

Convince someone of something today:

This is simple to consider, but somewhat more difficult to put into action. First of all, this must be a legitimate persuasion and not just getting someone to agree with you because you are the customer. It may take several attempts over the course of several days finally to accomplish the task. However, once accomplished, you will experience the confidence-building energy lift that comes from knowing that your powers of persuasion are improving. When you are in persuasive mode, you must pay special attention to the other person, you must adjust your tactics, listening very carefully to the body language and the other behavioral signals emitting from the person. Your intention to persuade becomes the engine driving the interaction, and as the conversation develops, you will find your attention taking on a unique quality. Gradually, over time, your onstage muscle of attention becomes even more effective and powerful.

Switch to non-dominant hand:

I'm stealing this from Jack Lemmon, who early in his career, while acting a somewhat unchallenging role in a television program, chose to make his character left-handed. The act of making himself use his non-dominant hand brought his performance to life, gave him a unique challenge, and stimulated his creativity.

Follow the gut, not the head:

Select a day to devote to only those tasks and actions that are dictated by the gut. No plans allowed. Arise when your inner clock dictates, eat only when and what your stomach asks for, walk to go only where you feel you are being guided, speak or not speak to others according to your gut level instinct and not according to social convention, family conditioning, or habit. Again, this exercise is not very difficult to understand intellectually, but considerably more difficult to accomplish in action.

The value of this exercise is extremely profound. First of all, it weans you from the entrenched habits you have been conditioned to use. It liberates the visceral gut-level language of the heart and soul. It can break down insecurities very quickly because very often the anxiety we experience is created by the conflict between what we think we should experience and what we actually experience.

When you go into a bookstore, for example, rather than heading toward your habitual area or for the promotional stacks, surrender to your instincts and go only where your gut tells you. Avoid undue analysis or the temptation to intellectualize your choices. Let this day be dedicated to following your instincts, whatever you do or do not do.

Naturally, you must defer to the safety voice within and maintain a modicum of reason and civility in order to avoid the kinds of mishaps that might derail your exercise. Keep it simple and unobtrusive. Over time, this exercise will integrate into your onstage awareness and will result in the kind of acting that can be considered truly alive, truly great.

A single day of completely clean:

This exercise is particularly useful for extending the actor's awareness of his or her basic habits, adds a special dimension of attention to each moment of the day, and exposes where the attention tends to slip or fall away. Choose a day of the week, perhaps the day on which you were born, and for two or three weeks in a row, dedicate that day to maintaining extraordinary cleanliness. Here's how this can manifest:

You are in a restaurant and go to the restroom. When you go to wash your hands you must insure that you avoid getting them contaminated again by touching the faucet handles when turning off the water, or the door-knob when leaving the restroom. In this scenario, you must assess the drying situation first. If it is paper towels, you must prepare the towels ahead of time, turn on the water, and wash your hands, use a paper towel to turn off the water and throw it away. Use a second paper towel to dry your hands. Use a third towel to turn the door knob and then while holding the door open with your shoulder or foot, you must toss the paper towel into the garbage bin and then exit. Then, upon returning to the table, you must take extra efforts to avoid touching chair backs or table tops, and so forth.

All of this must be done without anyone noticing the special effort. If you expose your game, you must abort and start again another day.

Inner Artifact

This is another private exercise. It makes use of the instrument's natural tendency to form habits. This exercise can be used to create vocal, physical, and psychological characteristics that are decidedly different from one's own collection of habits. By doing this, it follows the ancient concept of "new lamps for old."

There are two ways of approaching this; both are valid. One way asks that you, the actor, while in middle stages of character development, draw a number of abstract quick sketches that best depict the essence of the character. Next, pick one line or create a conglomerate line that seems to capture the basic spirit of the person you want to portray.

In the second approach, you examine a number of lines drawn on paper and pick one that stimulates your inner involvement. From this line, you can use this exercise to arrive at a unique characterization.

To begin, you take a fairly large drawing of the line (14 x 18 or larger), and pin it up on the wall in the work space. Once secured to the wall, the line should not be moved or altered for the duration of the session.

Next, stand in front of the drawing, and without moving the body begin to *breathe the line*. Softly inhale following the shape of the line, almost as if the line were entering the lungs. The exhale should follow the same pattern in reverse. Do this while looking at the line and listening for any inner feelings that may start to surface. This should continue, slowly and easily, for at least five minutes.

Gradually let the breath influence the movement of the head. Draw out the line with the head as you breathe the line. Let the facial features respond to the line as well. Draw with the eyes, nose, ears, tongue, every part. Keeping the breath connected to the movement, let this exploration filter down to include the shoulders, the arms, the hands, the chest, the waist, the hips, the pelvis, the knees, the ankles, and the toes.

After the entire body has had a chance to experience the line, stand still again and simply breathe it. As you do this, listen again for any feelings and let that influence the choice of what body part to move. Allow the breath to try out different tempos of the line as you explore the feeling with a single part of the body.

Begin to add the voice, softly at first. Let the voice follow the rhythm and feeling of the body. At this point, you can move away from the drawing and enter the space, allowing the movements more room and more dynamic.

As the exploration of the line continues, there may be moments of "double-think" or a sudden block. If this happens, and it is not uncommon, simply go back to the drawing and re-charge with a fresh look at the line. Once the mind is out of the way again, drift into the space with the voice and movements, exploring the line again and again.

Try not to force the exploration in a predetermined direction, let it take its own shape. Very often, during a line study of this nature, the actor will avoid going in directions that seem unrelated to the character he is working on. Keep in mind that an exploration is a journey into the *unknown* and as such should not be limited by preconceived notions of how the character is to be played. It is by having the courage to trust the uncharted territory that you can discover powerful character traits outside your personal bag of clichés.

After an unbridled exploration into the space with the voice and body, find the essential posture of the line. Exaggerate the posture and try a variety of walks, still following the dictates of the line. As the body walks the posture and rhythm of the line, begin to add a few words or phrases that seem to emerge from the exploration at this stage. Do not judge the content. What you say at this point is inconsequential; it is merely a first try at opening the psychology to the shape of the line.

This next phase of exploration is critical. By now you know how the line feels inside and how it manifests in gestures, posture, walk, and breath. Now begins the absorption of the line into the being.

Stand in the center of the space and begin to breathe the line again. Gradually form a pattern of movement that is generated from the breath. The pattern should involve as much of the body as possible and should be saturated with feeling. Repeat the pattern again and again at a comfortable dynamic until there is no question as to its complete shape.

Then, little by little, the pattern should increase in size and dynamic. You will begin to use more breath, more power, more space, making it larger and stronger in regular increments. This should build vocally as well. The pattern will expand in every way until you are using the entire room and are at the maximum level of vocal and physical dynamic.

Stay only momentarily at the peak and then begin to return in the same incremental manner. Step by step, the pattern will reduce in size and dynamic until, eventually, it will return to the comfortable level at which you began the crescendo. Do not stop here though. Let the line idle for a moment or two and then begin to diminish the dynamic, internalizing the pattern gradually.

Slowly, the pattern will become minute, the breath will be extremely small, and the pattern will have internalized to the degree that it will continue inside *with no outer manifestation*. At this point, the line has become a mantram, or inner artifact, that will begin to allow the character to emerge organically, from the inside.

Gestures, speech rhythms, movements of the eyes, the breath, the laugh, all aspects of the character will follow an essential code. At first it will need a bit of effort to sustain the connection to the artifact. Later on, it need only be activated with a thought, and then you are free to go on to more spontaneous acting dynamics, trusting that the character will now follow the new line of habits naturally, and any personal habits will be at a minimum.

The beauty of the technique is that it can be activated at a moment's notice and can also be dismissed with a quick command from the mind. It is useful for all styles of acting, for all characters, and does not interfere with the actor's need to be in the moment. More than that, it establishes a deeper level of trust in the actor's creative potential.

Village of the Idiots

This is one of my favorite exercises because it is so useful in introducing and playing out the fundamental idiocy of the human condition.

Start with participants on the floor, lying down on their backs. After a moment or two of relaxation, you welcome them to the "Idiots' Convention." They are all idiots at the convention and have somehow managed to get to this position on the floor. Their next mission is to get to a standing position. They must do this in the most idiotic fashion possible. Here's the way I usually narrate this—feel free to expand or improve upon it: "Now, without hurting yourself or anyone next to you, you must get to a stand in the most idiotic manner possible. There is no logic to this. It's ridiculous; makes no sense. OK ... and ... Go!"

Invariably, most of the group will begin doing the most outrageous and physically strenuous things possible. Let them go at it this way for a moment or two (as long as they are in no danger) and then stop the exercise to say the following: "OK, idiots, that was lovely. Except that a lot of you were using brute strength as your only means. Remember, there is no logic whatsoever. You may want to string yourself to a stand, or borrow the help of a pet mosquito, or become a fig tree, anything! If one attempt isn't successful, go to another one. Of course, none of them will succeed; but that shouldn't stop you from trying. OK, take a breath, ready, and Go!"

There is usually more invention at this stage and some of the attempts will be hilarious. I usually wait until I see a majority of interesting approaches and then yell "freeze." I then quickly ask each idiot, one at a time, to continue with his or her own attempt to stand. This gives the others a chance to see the variety of choices around them and further inspires a non-rational approach. I then encourage them really to believe that their way, regardless of how idiotic, will actually work for them.

After a minute or so, I tell them that their way is magically work-ing for them, and it will indeed allow them to get to a standing position. Once standing, I tell them that they are in a normal world all of a sud-den and that they want to try to appear normal. They must take their behavior from those around them. Whatever the others are doing must be "right" and "normal." I help guide this by interjecting comments like: "How are the others walking? What's the normal way to walk here?"

"How do people talk and communicate?"

"Stay alert, try to convince them that you are normal."

This follows its own course with people trying to discover the "right" way to sit down, to laugh, and to behave. It can release loads of inhibitions very quickly and helps people to see how social condi-tioning is a means of hiding the essential human comedy.

Plus, it's just plain fun. Those who jump into it and commit to the framework will be taken on a sublime ride into a dimension of com-munion and communication that will be both liberating and restrictive at the same time, a true paradox and a joy to behold.

Eventually, when the group seems to be nearing predictable or low energy, the "idiots" need to be invited to do the exact opposite: they are not to get caught doing ANYTHING the others are doing. If you see someone jumping, crawl, or if you see someone running, freeze, if nobody is making sound, sing out, and so forth, and so on. Eventually I tell them to freeze and dissolve to the floor, take a big breath, and then come out of it to talk and laugh about the experience. Again, great fun, zest for life, and resting in the fabric of shared experience.

Martha Graham 1968 *Eugene Gold*

E.J. Gold, Martha Graham, Pen and Ink, 1968,
signed L/R in ink Eugene Gold, 11" x 15", Rives
BFK, © 1968 Heidelberg Editions International.

CHAPTER SIXTEEN

CONCLUSION

I used the word "actor," but at a certain stage of human development the actor becomes an "agent," for he has come to realize that through him the purpose of the universe is indeed focused according to the time and place of his life performance. The ego in him has become a crystalline lens through which the "Will of God" is concentrated into individualized acts. He does not think; the One Mind thinks him. His life has become "sacred" because it is no longer "his" life, but the Whole performing within and through the space of his total organism, and at the time determined by the rhythm of the planetary process, whatever act is necessary.[1]

– Dane Rudhyar

The human dramas of this life-on-earth are most often performed by bumbling amateurs; people who have learned their roles half-heartedly. They stumble blindly from scene to scene, stealing focus and blowing lines, or missing entrances, hoping the playwright will fix things if they get in a bind. And they are always in a bind!

Then there are those humans who recognize the value of professional work. These beings study, observe, rehearse, investigate, and learn the lines necessary to get them through the labyrinthine story lines with grace and style. They are the wakeful ones, the passionate and inspired people who vitalize the world around them with their vigor, their authenticity and indomitable spirit. We learn from their adventures and sacrifice and benefit from the spiritual refinement they bring to their art.

Traditionally we associate those spiritually connected arts with visual art, poetry, dance, or music. Why should inspiration and growth in the spiritual dimension be relegated only to poets, musicians, painters, and dancers? The actor, too, has the right and the means to enter through the mysterious gates and struggle to awaken.

The theatre is an integral structure by nature, allowing each person who works within that world the opportunity to upgrade his or her professional skills, to grow through collaboration, and to evolve through the full spectrum of consciousness.

I challenge the new actor to join with the ancient actor and make even the smallest, most insipid assignment a spiritual task. Therein is the secret of overcoming the powerful current of mediocrity we now are facing. And perhaps, in time and with the help of all other workers in the spiritual dimension, there will be audiences who know how to digest what they are given. In those moments when the theatrical event is perceived as a possible vehicle of enlightenment, the art will have returned to its sacred function and actors will no longer need to "shop around" for spiritual guidance.

Until then, I suggest putting to work what can be gleaned from this text and beginning to match it with work that is in some way connected to a bona-fide tradition. Also, it can be very useful to form a group of fellow actors who are also searching for truth, and are willing to make a few sacrifices.

I do not know if the present surge in actor popularity will last. Hopefully, the flaky sensational aspects of the craft will diminish without actors losing the influence they now enjoy. The timing is critical, however, for if actors do not make the quantum leap in consciousness that other fields are making, actors in the 21st century will fall into another dark period, living as social outcasts. One can see glimmers of diminished power today as public consumption has embraced more and more "reality"-based television programming and more digital and animated projects compete for box office revenues. Fewer live theatres can support up-and-coming new playwrights. Add to that the fact that the greedy appetites for salacious news regarding the various escapades of celebrity actors have now created an atmosphere of derision toward most actors. The earlier view of acting as a discipline and a craft worthy of respect and honor has eroded considerably in recent years.

Acting, once a mysterious and sacred task is at risk of becoming a burlesque, a quaint endeavor from a by-gone era.

Do not allow this to happen. Take your nimble gifts and noble efforts into the crucible of the spirit. Emerge whole and clear-eyed as living examples of the new actor fearlessly participating in the full spectrum of human redemption—bringing light and joy to the hearts of many who thirst to awaken.

Do this and you shall be a friend to all humanity.

Finally, it is my most fervent wish that you translate this book into whatever personal language or spiritual filter is closest to your heart. I would only remind you to consider that all roads lead to Philadelphia (city of brotherly love). Take your road with gusto, kick up the dirt a little, gather friends who share your yearning, and move forward.

As you live each day and come to know, as I have, that we are all made of the same non-stuff; we are all constructed of vibration at various frequencies, and that, ultimately, this life is a fantastic parade of masks. Fear not, the old Hebrew question, "Of what did God make the world?" will eventually illuminate the very path on which you walk. I wish you well.

NOTES

Introduction

1.   Michael Talbot, *The Holographic Universe*
(HarperPerennial/HarperCollins,1991) pp. 12-32

Chapter One

(no notes)

Chapter II – History and the Craft of Acting

1.   Brian Bates, *The Way of the Actor*
(Boston: Shambhala Publications Inc.,1987) p.22

2.   Jeffrey Mishlove, *Roots of Consciousness*
(New York: Random House, New York, N.Y., 1975)
p.5

3.   Mircea Eliade, *Shamanism*
(Princeton: Princeton University Press, 1972) p.20

4. Larry Peters, "The Tamang Shamanism of Nepal",
    Chapter 10 in <u>Shamanism</u>, ed. by Shirley Nicholson
    (New York: Theosophical Publishing House, 1987)
    p.174

5. *ibid.*, pp.166-167

6. *ibid.*, p.85

7. Brian Bates, *The Way of the Actor*, p.22

8. Fred Mayer and Thomas Immoos, *Japanese Theatre*,
    trans. Hugh Young (Studio Vista, N.Y.: Rizzoli
    International Publications, 1977) p.38

9. *ibid.*, p.38

10. *ibid.*, p.38

11. Jeffrey Mishlove, *Roots of Consciousness*, p.22

12. "Delphi," *Encyclopedia Mythica* from *Encyclopedia
    Mythica Online*. pantheon.org/articles/d/delphi.html

13. Anthony J. Podlecki, *The Political Background of
    Aeschylean Tragedy* (University of Michigan Press,
    1966) p. 2

14. George Freedley and John A. Reeves, *A History of the
    Theatre* (New York: Crown Publishers, Inc.) p.13

15. Plato, *Five Great Dialogues*, trans. B. Jowett
    (New York: Walter J. Black Publishers, 1942) pp.31-65

16. Jeffrey Mishlove, *Roots of Consciousness*, p.23

17. *ibid.*, p.23

18.   Peter Brook, *The Empty Space*, p.62

19.   George Freedley and John A. Reeves, *A History of the
      Theatre* (New York: Crown Publishers, Inc.) p.
      62

20.   Russell Zguta, *Russian Minstrels* (Pittsburgh: Univ. of
      Pennsylvania Press,1978) p.101

21.   Frances A. Yates, *The Occult Philosophy in the
      Elizabethan Age* (London: Ark Paperbacks, 1979) p.70

22.   *ibid.*, pp.89-126

23.   *ibid.*, pp.159-163

24.   Elenor Fuchs, "The Mysterium: A Modern Dramatic
      Genre", Theatre Three, *Journal of Theatre & Drama of
      the Modern World* (Carnegie Mellon Univ., Fall 1986)
      pp.73-86

25.   Leo Shaya, *The Universal Meaning of the Kabbalah*,
      trans. Nancy Pearson (Baltimore, Maryland: Penguin
      Books Inc., 1973) pp.61-73

Chapter III – The Mystic Realist?

1.   P.D. Ouspensky, *In Search of the Miraculous*
      (New York: Harcourt Brace and Jovanovich, Inc., 1949)
      p.145

2.   Constantin Stanislavski, *An Actor Prepares*, trans.
      Elizabeth Hapgood (New York: Theatre Arts Books,
      1936) p.123

3.   Constantin Stanislavski, *On the Art of the Stage*, trans.

David Magarshack (N.Y.: Hill & Wang, 1961) p.164

4.   *ibid.*, p.169

5.   Susan G. Shumsky, *Chakras*,
        (New Page Books, 2003) pp.105-126

6.   Stanislavski, *An Actor Prepares*, p.187

7.   *ibid.*, p.187

8.   Constantin Stanislavski, *Building a Character*, trans.
        David Hapgood (New York: Theatre Arts Books, 1977)
        p.60

9.   Stanislavski, *An Actor Prepares*, p.271

Chapter IV – The Antidote to Narcissism

(no end notes)

Chapter V – The Tao of Acting

1.   William Shakespeare, *Hamlet – Act II, scene ii*

2.   James N. Powell, *The Tao of Symbols*
        (New York: Quill Press, 1982) p.124

3.   Benjamin Hoff, *The Tao of Pooh*
        (New York: E.P. Dutton Inc., 1982) p.10

Chapter VI – What is Going on Here?

1.   Itzak Bentov, *Stalking the Wild Pendulum*
        (New York: Bantam Books,1977) pp.25-26

2.   *ibid.*, p.38

3.   *ibid.*, pp.31-33

4.   Ouspensky, P.D., In Search of the Miraculous, pp. 181-198

Chapter VII – The Challenge of Awakening

1.   Bill Harris, *Thresholds of the Mind*
        (Centerpoint Press, 2002) pp.16-37

2.   E. J. Gold, *The Joy of Sacrifice – Secrets of the Sufi Way*
        (IDHHB, Inc. and Hohm press, 1978) pp.4-13

3.   Bill Harris, *Thresholds of the Mind*
        (Centerpoint Press, 2002) p.42

4.   Daniel Goleman, *Varieties of the Meditative Experience*
        (New York: E. Dutton, 1977) p.56

5.   E.J. Gold, *Practical Work on Self*
        (Gateways/IDHHB, Inc., 1992) p.3

6.   E.J. Gold, *The Human Biological Machine as a
        Transformational Apparatus*
        (Gateways/IDHHB Publishers, 1985) pp.45-46

Chapter VIII – Higher Bodies

1.   Bentov, op.cit., pp. 13-139

2.   Hua-Ching, Ni, *The Taoist Inner View of the Universe
        and the Immortal Realm* (The Shrine of the Eternal
        Breath of Tao Press, 1979) pp.142-149

3.   P.D. Ouspensky, *In Search of the Miraculous*, p.180

4.   Brian Bates, *The Way of the Actor*
        (Shambhala Press, 2001) pp.175-178

5.   Wilder Penfield and Phanor Perot, *Brain Vol. 86, Part
        Dec. 1963 The Brain's Record of Auditory and Visual
        Experience*, pp.613-645

6.   Ken Wilber, *Sex, Ecology, Spirituality*
        (Shambhala Publications, Inc. 1998) pp.215-216

Chapter IX – Higher Purpose

1.   Z'ev Ben Shimon Halevi, *Kabbalah and Exodus*
        (Boulder: Shambhala Press,1980) p.43

2.   Bentov, *op. cit.*, p.184

Chapter X – Mindfulness and Acting

1.   Lama Anagarika Govinda, *Creative Meditation and
        Multidimensional Consciousness* (New York:
        Questbook,Theosophical Publishing, 1973)
        p.125

2.   Edward Marsel, *The Resurrection of the Body – the
        Essential Writings of F. M. Alexander* (Boston:
        Shambhala Press, 1969) p.11

3.   *ibid.*, p.8

4.   William Shakespeare, *The Tempest,* Act IV , i. 148
        (Prospero)

5.   Thomas Merton, *The Asian Journal* (New York: New Directions Journal Publishing, 1973) p. 401

6.   Brad Darrach, "Meryl Streep – On Top and Tough Enough to Stay There" (*Life Magazine*, Dec. 1987, Vol. 10,#13) pp.72-82

Chapter XI – Gateways

1.   Hua-Ching, Ni, *The Taoist Inner View of the Universe and the Immortal Realm*, p.68

2.   Halevi, *Kabbalah and Exodus*, p.199

3.   Michael Chekhov, *To the Actor* (New York: Harper & Row, 1953) p.12

4.   Ken Wilber, *Sex, Ecology, Spirituality*, pp.59-61

5.   Ajat Mookerjee and Jadhu Khanna, *The Tantric Way*, (London: Little Brown and Co. Ltd., 1986) p.23

6.   Helevi, *op cit.*, p.200

7.   Fred Gettings, *The Encyclopedia of the Occult* (London: Rider and Co. Ltd., 1986)

Chapter XII – Sexual Energy and Acting

1.   Da Love Ananda, *The Eating Gorilla Comes in Peace* (San Rafael: The Free Daist Communion and the Dawn Horse Press, 1987) pp.331-345

2.   Ken Wilber, *Sex, Ecology, Spirituality*, pp.634-637

Chapter XIII – Not Me, Not Not Me

1.   Richard Schechner, *Between Theatre and Anthropology* (Philadelphia: Univ. Pennsylvania Press, 1985) pp.248-49

Chapter XIV – Words of Warning

1.   E.J. Gold, *The Joy of Sacrifice* – Secrets of the Sufi Way, pp.16-33

2.   Bentov, *Stalking the Wild Pendulum*, pp.224-225

3.   St. John of the Cross, *Dark Night of the Soul*, trans. Kurt Reinhardt (New York, Frederick Ungar Pub.,1957) p.33

Chapter XV – Practical Exercises

1.   William Shakespeare, *A Midsummer Night's Dream*, Act II, i.

Conclusion

1.   Dane Rudhyar, *An Astrological Mandala* (New York: Vintage Books, 1974) p.34

Mark Olsen Photograph by Kevin Fox

ABOUT THE AUTHOR

MARK OLSEN

Mark Olsen is an actor, director, author, and teacher. Currently a professor of acting and movement at the Penn State School of Theatre, Mr. Olsen has taught at other notable institutions such as Carnegie Mellon University, University of Houston, Ryerson Theatre School in Toronto and New York Public Theatre's Shakespeare Lab. Specializing in empowering students to devise original works for stage and screen, Mark has been a frequent guest director and teacher for Bucknell University, Central Connecticut University, Webster Movement Institute, and the National Fight Director's Workshop for the Society of American Fight Directors (S.A.F.D.) He has appeared on Broadway and toured Internationally with the famed mime/mask group, *Mummenschanz*, and acted in numerous regional theatre productions. Olsen played the title character in the independent film, *Rocky Road*, and has worked on several film and television projects including *Woman of Independent Means* starring Sally Field, John Slattery, and Tony Goldwyn. He has directed over forty-five productions in both professional and university settings and has worked as movement coordinator and fight director for numerous productions at the Houston Shakespeare Festival, Hartford Stage Company, Theatreworks, The Alley Theatre, Houston Grand Opera, New York Shakespeare Festival, and New York's Public Theatre. Mark is a nationally recognized authority on movement and stage combat, as well as an A.E.A. actor, certified teacher and former secretary of S.A.F.D., and former vice-president of the Association for Theatre Movement Educators. Mr. Olsen has taught his unique approach to theatre and spiritual development at the Esalen Institute, the Omega Institute, The New York Open Center and the Institute for the Development of the Harmonious Human Being. Mark's exciting approach to acting incorporates classical and contemporary techniques developed through the comprehensive lens of the Ken Wilber Integral Theory. In addition to his theatre experience, Mark has worked with many of the world's renowned spiritual teachers including Taoist master Donkuk Ahn, modern Sufi master E.J. Gold, Kabbalist Samuel Avital, Brazilian mystic Ivaldo Bertozzi, and Kung Fu artist Jeff Bolt. Other books by Mr. Olsen include, *The Actor with a Thousand Faces* and *The Conception Mandala* (co-authored with Samuel Avital).

INDEX

LETTER TO THE READER

Gateways is pleased to present for you Mark Olsen's revised first book. We are proud to continue publishing his work for you, whether you are a theatre professional, an initiate on a spiritual path, or simply an adventurous reader.

If you wish to contact Mark regarding his current workshop and lecture schedule - or his availability for any training event related to the ideas in *The Golden Buddha Changing Masks* – write to him c/o Gateways at the address given below.

Gateways also produces an extensive line of high-quality books as well as audio tapes, CDs, DVDs, and videos. Their subject matter is practical spiritual work, transformation, and advanced coursework both for inner awakening and for artistic applications of these ideas.

For a current catalog, write or call us at the following address/phone:

GATEWAYS PUBLISHING / IDHHB, Inc.
P. O. Box 370
Nevada City, California 95959-0370
800-869-0658 530-271-2239
gatewaysbooksandtapes.com idhhb.com